PRAISE FOR THE ENG@GED CUSTOMER

"When I first saw what the team at Post Communications was doing several years ago, I returned to Palm and told my colleagues that I had seen the future of direct marketing. I was right, and now Hans Peter Brondmo has taken the learning and insight from Post and written an indispensable guide for any marketer, describing how to harness the incredible power and avoid the pitfalls of direct marketing with e-mail."

—ANDREA BUTTER
Former vice president, marketing, of Palm, Inc.
Author of *Piloting Palm*

"Hans Peter Brondmo is the undisputed visionary in his field."

—GEOFFREY MOORE, president, The Chasm Group
Author of *Crossing the Chasm, Inside the Tornado, The Gorilla Game,* and *Living on the Fault Line*

"The Internet creates new opportunities for every company to deliver value to its customers. Listening to customers and structuring communications around their needs can turn a marketing nuisance e-mail into a welcome source of information. From the earliest days of the World Wide Web, Hans Peter Brondmo has been a pioneer and thought-leader focused on the customer's perspective. I recommend you read this book to understand how your company can use e-mail to form high-quality customer relationships with the power to transform your business."

—JOY COVEY
Ex chief financial officer and chief strategy officer, Amazon.com

"We bought Hans Peter's company, Post Communications, because it is the clear thought leader in Internet direct marketing. Now that thinking and the experience behind it is available to you. This book is a must read if you've ever worried about how to stay in touch with your customers in the new economy."

—WEST SHELL III
CEO and chairman, Netcentives, Inc.

"As we move into the twenty-first century, it is clear that there is a shift of power from producers of goods and retailers toward their customers. The Internet provides a marketplace for both businesses and consumers that erases geography and is on all the time. With this revolution comes opportunity. *The Eng@ged Customer* not only makes light of this shift in power but instructs businesses in how to take advantage of it."

—JONATHAN NELSON
CEO, Organic, Inc.

"There is a world of difference between managing customers as part of a relational database and treating customers as part of a real relationship. Relationship management online is not merely value-added information management. That's why this book will become even more important as Net technologies evolve."

—MICHAEL SCHRAGE
Codirector, MIT Media Lab's eMarkets Initiative, and author of *Serious Play*

"Hans Peter Brondmo knows more about marketing on the Internet than almost anyone alive today. This book is essential reading for anyone who wants to learn from a master."

—SETH GODIN
Author of *Permission Marketing*

"If you care about acquiring and retaining customers in the e-world, this is a book you can put to use immediately and keep coming back for more! Hans Peter Brondmo has it just right: success in electronic commerce and e-business is not about marketing but about creating ongoing relationships with your customers."

—PATRICIA B. SEYBOLD
CEO, The Patricia Seybold Group
Author of *Customers.com*

"One unavoidable truth about the Internet: Every man, woman and child on the planet will soon have an e-mail address. Hans Peter Brondmo has written the definitive guide for using e-mail as a cornerstone for your customer marketing and relationship development. Any CEO worth his salt, dot com or traditional, should keep this book on his desk!"

—STEWART ALSOP
Partner, New Enterprise Associates, and columnist, *Fortune* Magazine

"Wegmans has been building relationships with customers for half a century. This book shows established companies like ours how to use the Internet to enhance these relationships and "engage" customers in a deeper, value-enhancing, online dialogue. It is a must read for any executive concerned about the impact of the Internet on his or her business."

—STEVE MICHAELSON
Vice president marketing, Wegmans Food Markets

"This is the ultimate one-to-one marketing. Brondmo teaches how digital technology enables companies to reach a global market in small, down-home ways. Fast, localized, and personalized—but on a global scale."

—JON NORDMARK
President and CEO, eBags.com

"In a world where the Internet has changed the "art of the possible" in marketing faster than most businesses have adapted, Brondmo offers practical and timely perspectives on how to be effective with what has to be a cornerstone of almost every marketer's going-forward program."

—MARC SINGER
Principal and coleader of CRM practice, McKinsey & Company
Coauthor of *Net Worth*

"Hans Peter Brondmo delivers both the theory and roadmap for developing e-mail strategies that create long-term, one-to-one Learning Relationships with valuable customers."

—DON PEPPERS AND MARTHA ROGERS, PH.D.
Partners, Peppers and Rogers Group

THE
ENG@GED
CUSTOMER

THE
ENG@GED
CUSTOMER

THE NEW RULES
OF INTERNET
DIRECT MARKETING

HANS PETER BRONDMO

HARPERBUSINESS
An Imprint of HarperCollins*Publishers*

To THE MEMORY OF MY FATHER

GUNNAR BRONDMO

HarperCollins books may be purchased for educational, business, or sales promotional use. For information please write: Special Markets Department, HarperCollins Publishers, Inc., 10 East 53rd Street, New York, NY 10022.

FIRST EDITION

Designed by Michael Mendelsohn at MM Design 2000, Inc.

Library of Congress Cataloging-in-Publication Data

Brondmo, Hans Peter.
    The eng@ged customer : the new rules of Internet direct marketing / Hans Peter Brondmo.
        p.   cm.
    Includes index.
    ISBN 0-06-662078-3
    1. Internet marketing.   I. Title: The eng@ged customer.   II. Title.

HF5415.1265 .B76 2000
658.8'4—dc21   00-040932

00 01 02 03 04 RRD 10 9 8 7 6 5 4 3 2 1

CONTENTS

FOREWORD

GEOFFREY MOORE

IN PICKING UP THIS BOOK to learn more about email-based marketing, you have put yourself in extremely good hands. As a colleague and an investor in Post Communications, the company he founded, I know of no one more qualified to tackle this job than Hans Peter Brondmo. As you read through his book, you will find that, in fact, it is a *twofer*: both a thoughtful discussion of the why's of email direct marketing and a highly pragmatic discourse on the how's. All in all, a great value.

But there is more to it than that. This book is timely in a sense that few books are. We are on the cusp of a change in marketing that is so far-reaching we cannot yet fathom its scope. We know the underpinnings, to be sure. We know that the Internet puts the customer in control of the email relationship in a way that was never before possible. We know that for the first time we have an opportunity to conduct dialogue with our customers on a massive scale. We know that during the moment of customer service, we can call up all the information we have about a customer in order to create a more satisfying experience. And we now recognize that the value of keeping a satisfied, loyal customer is significantly greater than chasing one who comes and goes.

We know all these things and a host of other related ideas and data. What we do not know yet is what they really mean. It is simply too soon to know, but perhaps not too soon to speculate. That, at any rate, is my intention in this foreword.

Throughout my business career, marketing communications has

been framed as a competition with other vendors to gain the attention of prospective customers. It has been an exercise in cutting through the noise with a message pretuned to some wavelength in the prospective customer's mind that lets it pass through a myriad of defense mechanisms to increase receptivity and evoke a response. Of course, any message that actually works gets copied, and so prospective clients quickly learn to tune out that wavelength as well, and the search for some newer one commences. Except for the feedback of focus groups, which can be notoriously misleading, we are essentially flying blind throughout the process.

This exercise defines *communicating* as transmission and stimulation—the outbound sending of a message to evoke a response. As this book makes clear, in the age of the Internet we have the opportunity—and, over time, the requirement—to redefine the direction of communication as inbound, an act of reception, where the one stimulated to action is not the prospect but ourselves. We must, in short, reinvent our companies as vending machines.

A vending machine exposes itself through a user interface that offers to prospective customers a set of controls by which they can manipulate the machine to fulfill their desires. People love this convention. Given the choice between being served by a human being or a well-designed machine, people choose the latter: this is the lesson of the ATM machine. At the other end of the spectrum, however, is the curse of being ill-served by a poorly designed machine, leading people to contemplate assassinations and bombings: this is the lesson of being stuck in voicemail jail, enduring an unending list of perpetually deferred outcomes, none of which maps to what one really wants or needs.

In the economy of the Internet, Darwinian competition will promote companies with well-designed interfaces and eliminate the others. Based upon word of mouth or buyer ratings, people will point each other to the satisfying experiences and post "Out of Order" signs on the offending sites.

So which are you going to be? This greatly depends on the management style of your company. Prior to the age of the Internet, competition rewarded companies with aggressive outbound selling styles led by people who took control of the selling situation early and drove it to closure. These folks treat selling as hunting and see themselves as carnivores stalking their rightful victims. The last thing that would occur to them is to set up a self-service bar for their prey.

Nothing has changed to prevent the hunting style of selling from continuing to deliver results. All that has changed is that a cheaper, more intimate, and potentially more loyalty-inducing venue for customer relationships has emerged. Companies able to leverage this new venue should be able to outperform their hunter-competitors by securing deeper customer relationships that inspire not only more follow-on business, thereby more than offsetting the cost of customer acquisition, but also active recruiting of additional new prospects at no additional marketing cost. Over time, as the hunters venture out repeatedly to find new prospects—since their style of selling creates a residue of ill will that makes repeat business improbable—the economic advantage of a service culture becomes increasingly competitive.

That, at any rate, is the theory, which at present is unproven. As a result, committing the corporation to this approach is risky. So what kind of management team is going to take this risk, and what kind of management style is needed to be successful in so doing?

Our work at The Chasm Group on the dynamics of adopting new technologies tells us that two types of management teams will engage at this time. The first are visionaries who see where the future trend is headed and act to intercept it. Their goal is to leapfrog the competition by being the first in their competitive set to move onto the new platform, thereby gaining first-mover advantage. Today's automobile industry is ripe for such first movers, as visionary management realizes that gaining a long-term customer service relationship is more valuable than any short-term gain in price manipulation.

The second are pragmatists in pain who see their present situation as so grim that embracing unproven alternatives looks better than sticking with the status quo. Their goal is to escape their current dilemma as quickly as possible. The office products industry fits this profile because competition in what are essentially commodity goods has driven down their margins to near zero. By gaining a relationship with a customer, it can secure an increasing amount of ancillary purchases, resulting in higher profit margins—provided, that is, that it can identify the special offers that this customer will perceive as worth the "little bit extra" it expends. In an increasingly commoditized market, companies live or die based on their ability to garner that little bit extra.

So either you are moving ahead of the herd for competitive advantage, or you—along with your competitors—are remaining behind together in order to escape what is indeed presently painful. In either case, what type of management style is needed to succeed? Recall that your task is to transform your company into a vending machine. What does that really take?

Fundamentally, it takes a service culture that genuinely puts the customer first in any thought process. You actually have to redesign your entire operation from the outside in, first specifying the customer experience at the interface, then assembling the resources needed to make that experience happen. Let me just say flat out that a more unnatural act you will never perform. That is, when you go to make this happen, do not be surprised to find everything in the wrong place. Companies evolve from the inside out, not the other way around, and what makes life easy for the customer makes it challenging for the vendor. As soon as you embrace the customer view, you are letting yourself in for a real challenge.

The companies best able to master this challenge are those willing to fake it at the outset. At Mohr Davidow Ventures, where we invested in Post Communications and in Hans Peter's talents, we call this "Ozzing." Basically, winning companies act like the Wizard of Oz, doing whatever it takes behind the scenes in order to create the powerful effects desired. If this means letting people order over the Internet, only to rekey the order into some in-house ERP system, so be it. If it means calling by phone or sending a fax in order to provide backup to an email, so be it. In the long term such tactics are prohibitively uneconomical, but in the short term the only uneconomical outcome is losing a relationship with a prospective customer or establishing the wrong expectation about your customer service promise.

Companies that have a bottom-line style have real trouble with Ozzing precisely because it violates their cardinal rule against being inefficient and overly expensive. Companies that want a "perfect system" up and running before they release it to the pubic also have trouble. They typically already have well-established customer relationships and are hesitant to put them at risk through a new technology. The problem is that in battles for market share in emerging markets, time is at least as precious an asset as cash, and not getting in early can lead to being only a me-too offer by the time you do get there. It is therefore important for the management team to look down the road, see the investment needed, and then decide up front whether it is willing to pay the price. No one is served by an Internet strategy that gets lip service in the boardroom but is undermined in the field.

In closing, my hope is that your company meets the market profile of an early adopter of Internet direct marketing and that your management style permits you to engage in this new discipline immediately and aggressively. If so, you will be deeply grateful to the author for having written this book. It offers a clear explanation of the dynamics of email relationship marketing as well as a terrific how-to guide for incorporating the new tools and processes into an existing marketing operation. If you are going down this path, I encourage you to make it mandatory reading company-wide to ensure that everyone gets a head start on the right path.

ACKNOWLEDGMENTS

A LTHOUGH MY NAME APPEARS on the cover, this book had its origins in the inspiration, support, thoughts, ideas, and hard work contributed by a large number of people with whom I have had the great fortune to collaborate over the years. A few pages of text can hardly do them the justice they deserve, but I nevertheless want to acknowledge some of the most important contributors.

Susan and Gunnar Brøndmo started it all. My mother and father's love, support, and enthusiasm for my many adventures and endeavors taught me that I can think that which is not commonly thought and do that which is not commonly done. Thank you.

The work and insights that inform most of this book come from the company I founded in 1996, Post Communications, Inc., and from our clients. Although the book is not about Post, I have relied heavily on the insight that working with our clients has taught me. I was able to start Post primarily because of a few people. Jonathan Harber helped give me the freedom to dabble and taught me a thing or two about making something from nothing. Peter Barrett introduced me to Jonathan Feiber of Mohr Davidow Ventures, who realized that there "was a pony in there somewhere" and stuck with us. Post would not have happened without John R. Ellis, my brilliant (and strong-willed) technical cofounder. Pål Roppen and the early-stage investors helped get the ball rolling. The founding team members deserve much credit: Peter Kovac, Joe Stampleman, Leah Edwards, Ed Henrich, Jim Macinnes, Mary Long, and Ana Witherow, among others. Denise Thomas helped give much of the preliminary thinking some form. Cheryl Vedoe's helmsmanship at Post and support for the book has made it possible for me to dedicate the significant time and resources necessary to write *The Eng@ged Customer*.

The proof is as always in the pudding. And in this instance the "pudding" is provided by the people and companies that have become Post's clients. Thanks to all of them for their willingness and enthusiasm to discover and chart new territory with us. Special credit goes to Andrea Butter and the teams at Palm Inc.; David Pakman at N2K and the teams at N2K and CDNOW; Jon Nordmark and Larry Martine at eBags; Fred Berns and his team at Victoria's Secret. Thanks also to all of Post's clients.

Murray Brozinsky at Netcentives helped formulate ideas and contributed the "return on loyalty" (ROL) model. Jim Manzi, at Applied Predictive Technologies, contributed the predictive model comparison chart. Jeff Snedden and Bob Kestenbaum helped influence my thinking at an important juncture.

My agent, Jim Levine, walks on water. Without Jim and his team at James Levine Communications this book would be a shadow of itself. Thanks to Geoff Moore for the introduction and support. Armin Brott helped super-edit to make it all eminently more understandable and readable. Thank you to Dave Conti, Adrian Zackheim, Lisa Berkowitz, Michelle Jacob, and the rest of the folks at HarperBusiness for their enthusiasm, support, and patience.

The following people should be mentioned for the help, input, and support they provided: Tammy Ziehm, Erica Blue, Adam Gayner, Jim Kelly, Christopher Stathousis, Angelique Tober, Laura Lee, Hillary New, Amber Hanlin, Jennifer Lancaster, Irina Doliov, Stacy Smith, Jeff Houser, Mandy Dean, Teresa Puentes, David McKay, Bruce Sattley, Mary Regan, Andrea Grindeland, Alison Pazourek, Wendy Tacquard, Peter Cobb, Steve Michaelson, Chris Hoerenz, Joanna Gallanter, West Shell, Jonathan Nelson, and Michael Solomon. I apologize to those I have inadvertantly left out. I know there are many.

Last, but certainly not least, my thanks and tremendous appreciation go to Julie Hanna Farris. Without your love, encouragement, and support, my life as a first-time author would simply have been unbearable.

Hans Peter Brondmo

INTRODUCTION

I MAGINE YOU RUN a company that just spent $10 million on marketing and advertising to acquire its first 200,000 Internet customers. You've been running television, radio, and print ads, you've built a public relations machine, you've joined affiliate marketing programs, you have banners all over the Web, and you have partnerships with more companies than you can be expected to remember. So far you have lost more money than you're comfortable talking about. Oh, and let's not forget Wall Street has decided that losing money alone isn't a sustainable business any longer, whether your business name ends with ".com" or not. Now what?

Many of the rules on the Internet are different, but the business fundamentals are very similar: If your customers aren't buying from you, they're clicking over to someone else—something that gets easier every day. So how do you increase their switching costs so they'll stay engaged with you after making that first purchase? How do you determine which customers you want to keep and which ones are less important? How do you avoid spam—the unwanted, unsolicited, unexpected, and soon-to-be-unlawful junk mail of the Internet—and the potential nightmares of privacy violations? How do you rise above the increasing clutter and noise and become the trusted voice that your customers rely on?

After reading this book you will gain insight into powerful strategies and hands-on tactics for turning those 200,000 initial buyers into profitable, loyal, and engaged customers. I begin by pointing to the obvious: Central to any healthy relationship is good communication. The relationships you develop with your Internet customers must be based on open and honest communication guided by the "online service imperative." Customers don't want to have *marketing* relationships with your company; they want to have a *service* relationship. The key to successful Internet direct marketing and to establishing valuable customer relationships is to establish individualized service-based communication with each and every prospect and customer. The best tool that has ever existed for establishing this type of communication is the Internet, or, more precisely, *email.*

EMAIL—SIMPLY POWERFUL
YET EXCEPTIONALLY COMPLEX

While on the surface it may seem fairly simple to use email to communicate with your customers, online retailers and marketers all over the country have been discovering that it is very difficult to do well. Back in 1997, Palm Inc. was the first to enunciate an important industry realization: "We have several hundred thousand customers in our Internet database and there are millions more we'd like to get in touch with, but we don't know who they are and we don't know how to communicate effectively with them. Plus, we're worried about privacy issues and spam."

It was obvious that email could, should, and someday would be a useful tool for building a dialogue with customers. But email was a new and different medium, without established rules or conventions. And neither executives nor marketing managers—whether at traditional brick-and-mortar or pure-play Internet companies—knew quite what to do with this huge opportunity that was staring them in the face. The executives were looking for a high-level framework to help them think strategically, to figure out where and how to invest in building a successful Internet direct marketing program, and even to define what success would mean. Just down the hall in the very same organizations, marketing managers were being asked to run tactical, promotional email campaigns and to design retention-based email marketing programs. In many cases they were flying blind and needed best-practice guidelines and concrete examples. *The Eng@ged Customer* satisfies both these needs, providing a comprehensive strategic framework as well as a solid set of tactical implementation tools.

INTERNET MARKETING AND SELLING IS COMING OF AGE

There is no longer a debate about whether people will choose to make their purchases online. In 1999 Amazon.com alone brought in well over $1 billion in revenue, selling a range of generally low-cost items. At the other end of the spectrum, BMW of North America discovered that 90 percent of its customers use the Internet before making their final decision to purchase a new BMW. And there's no end in sight: Forrester Research predicts that by the year 2003 business-to-consumer (B2C) sales online will exceed $144 billion, while business-to-business (B2B) sales will top $1.3 trillion.

To position itself to take advantage of this explosive growth, the (fictional) company you run (the one with 200,000 customers) is making huge investments to build brand awareness and attract new customers. But as the world of e-commerce rapidly matures, you are realizing that if you want to survive online, you're going to have to shift much of your focus from acquiring new customers to retaining them. How? By engaging customers in a dialogue and by building lasting, service-oriented relationships. And email is the most effective means to that end.

Whether you're sending individual customers their stock portfolio update at the end of each trading day, writing a gossip column on the music industry, sending special offers or promotions, publishing an industry newsletter, sending a purchase confirmation, or running a gift reminder-and-product-suggestion service, email marketing can do the job. Email is the strategic marketing tool that the leading customer-focused organizations will use to establish profitable relationships based on ongoing communication with their most valuable customers when selling online and, in many cases, offline.

LEARNING FROM THE LEADERS
AND THE INNOVATORS

Over the last few years, my colleagues and I at Post Communications have had the good fortune to work with a number of pioneering e-marketing and e-retailing firms to design and implement their industry-leading email direct marketing programs. You'll probably be very familiar with some of them: Victoria's Secret, OfficeMax, Harlequin Enterprises Limited, Hewlett Packard, Wegmans Food Markets, Amtrak, and CDNOW. Others, such as Women.com, CareGuide, Homestore.com, SelfCare, MyPlay, iOwn, eBags, Sparks.com, wildbrain.com, WineShopper.com, and Petopia don't have the same level of name recognition yet, but they are rapidly becoming established leaders in their categories as they redefine retail and service through the Internet. Throughout this book you'll find examples that illustrate how these early innovators and leaders have navigated the uncharted waters of Internet direct marketing, engaging their customers and members in lasting dialogue and establishing deep loyalty along the way.

As with most innovations on the Internet, email marketing is closely tied to technological research and development, which in turn enable companies to use email to establish highly automated yet individualized communication with thousands or even millions of customers. Although this book is not specifically about the technology of email marketing, my background and that of the team of brilliant technologists I've had the good fortune to work with over the past several years have enabled us to push the boundaries not only of the *theory* of Internet direct marketing, but of the *practical realities* of the field as well. As you read this book, you'll learn how Internet direct marketing and the technology of the Internet go hand in hand, and you'll develop a solid understanding of the opportunities—and the stumbling blocks—that lie ahead.

HOW TO GET THE MOST OUT OF THIS BOOK

The Eng@ged Customer is really two books in one: a guide to thinking and a guide to doing. It's organized into four parts. If you are an executive looking for an overview of how email marketing will impact your business, you'll want to read Parts I and IV carefully and skim Parts II and III. If you are a manager responsible for implementing and operating email marketing programs, you'll probably want to read the entire book, focusing especially on Parts II and III. But before you commit to either of these options, take a minute to read the following descriptions of each part.

PART I: USING EMAIL TO ENGAGE YOUR CUSTOMERS

The Internet is a new medium that requires many of the traditional principles and proven methodologies from the offline world to be carefully reconsidered. Nevertheless, I begin the book by suggesting that we return to some age-old principles at the core of which are personal service and communication. I then outline the factors that make it not only possible but necessary to engage your customers in an ongoing dialogue through email. I provide a brief historical backdrop, looking at email marketing in the context of the evolution of e-marketing. While email holds incredible promise, there are some clouds on the horizon in terms of declining response rates and increasing sensitivity to spam. I present an overview of the email marketing landscape as it exists today, which ranges from spam to opt-in email to customer dialogue and service. Finally, I consider some important factors that are shaping how we market online: culture, technology, the nature of the medium, and economics. Online businesses will survive and thrive only by building trust-based relationships with their customers. Those that don't will have no future in the customer-centric and customer-driven world of the Internet.

PART II: TAKING A STRATEGIC APPROACH

I begin this part by outlining the many applications of email marketing, from customer acquisition, to conversion, to retention and loyalty programs. I then describe how to clearly define goals and objectives for your Internet direct marketing programs, as well as how to use these goals to develop return-on-investment scenarios. Careful planning is key to a successful program design and implementation. I next outline some useful ways to keep your programs on track and on budget, such as developing a customer contact plan and a detailed roadmap. Throughout this part I examine what we can learn—as well as what we should forget—from traditional direct marketing and how email must be integrated with all marketing and customer communication programs across all channels. Because data drives how relevant your communication can be and relevance drives response and engagement, I devote the final chapter of this section to a discussion of the importance, power, and pitfalls of customer data. I also describe how to develop customer data models and contact strategies that successfully leverage that data.

PART III: IMPLEMENTING CUSTOMER DIALOGUE

This part contains all the information and tools necessary to kick off an email marketing program. It's where we roll up our sleeves and get to work. I start with a deeper look into some of the foundation elements I covered in earlier chapters, such as how to actually get to know each customer, what the life cycle of a customer relationship is, and how to consider automating the customer dialogue. I also discuss the 12 best practices for email relationship marketing. I then move onto a thorough, hands-on discussion of how to get an email marketing program up and running (including specifics on how to implement an individualized contact plan and how to evaluate each component you'll need to design, implement, and operate your program). Since email marketing has very different criteria for measuring and tracking success than traditional offline marketing, I dedicated an entire chapter to this very issue. I conclude this section with a who's who in the world of Internet direct marketing, which will help you by developing a framework for evaluating the players you may want to work with to build and execute your Internet direct marketing programs.

PART IV: LOOKING AHEAD

I begin this final part by discussing the implications email-based customer marketing and communication may have for your organization. What should you plan for as you consider the future? Where is the field of electronic customer communication and marketing headed? Which conceptual and technical developments will drive change? I take a look at whether government should regulate how companies use customer information or whether the current industry "self-regulation" initiatives will suffice. Finally, I present a vision of the future that moves beyond email into a world where your mobile telephone, television, dishwasher, sprinkler system, and car are all connected to the Internet. Each of these innovations—and many, many others—will have a powerful impact and broad implications on the ways companies communicate with their customers and their members.

I trust you will conclude that this book offers a helpful strategic vision for navigating the constantly changing landscape of the world of Internet marketing. By implementing the strategies and principles outlined in this book, you'll be able to start using Internet Direct Marketing to its fullest potential, which will drive your company's growth and increase the long-term value of each and every customer. In short, whether you're an executive or a manager, whether you focus on marketing or technology, by the time you're through reading *The Eng@ged Customer* you'll have the knowledge you need to stop losing sleep over how to keep your customers coming back in a medium where *they* are in control and where it's getting harder every day to rise above the clutter and noise to truly differentiate yourself and your company.

PART I

USING EMAIL TO ENGAGE YOUR CUSTOMERS

CHAPTER 1

BACK TO THE FUTURE

I T MAY SOUND ODD, but the Holy Grail of Internet commerce and marketing is to provide the same kind of service that merchants and storekeepers did about a hundred years ago. At the turn of the last century, if you were a good customer your butcher might set aside his best cut of meat for you. He knew your tastes, your preferences, perhaps even how many family members you were buying for and whether any of them had special dietary needs. He might even suggest a few recipes every once in a while.

Customers—whether they're buying online or walking into a store—have always patronized companies that offer good products and services. But that has never been all there is to a purchase decision—and the old-time butcher knew it. He understood four basic principles: *recognize and greet every customer by name, communicate with each one as an individual, reward the best customers, and provide great service to everyone.* Consumers responded accordingly, giving their business to companies that recognized them, respected their time and privacy, simplified their choices, knew when to talk and when to listen, and engaged them in open, honest communication.

But in the era of mass merchandising and mass marketing, getting to know every customer and interact with each one individually

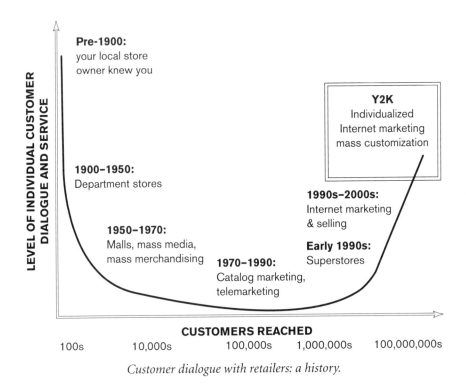

Customer dialogue with retailers: a history.

is a financial near-impossibility, especially if you've got tens or hundreds of thousands—perhaps even millions—of customers.

As we look at the history of retailing and customer marketing over the past one hundred years, it's clear that there's a direct link between technological innovation and change in retail. Incredible improvements in manufacturing, transportation, and communication technologies made three things happen. First, manufacturing made it possible to produce and distribute an enormous range of new products with incredible efficiency. Second, new forms of transportation and communication allowed consumers to travel greater distances to shop or even transport goods directly to consumers. The railroad made it possible to open the first department stores at the turn of the last century. Goods could be manufactured at geographically remote locations and transported by train in large volumes and at reasonable costs to the department stores. Customers, in turn, could jump on a local passenger train or streetcar and go shopping downtown. A few decades later the automobile made it feasible to build big malls outside of the town center, where there was ample and cheap real estate. New forms of communications technologies had eliminated distance as an important factor in where and how people could shop. Credit cards were invented in the 1950s, and toll-free 800 telephone numbers were introduced in the late 1970s. Both these advances gave catalog and telephone shopping and marketing a huge boost. But even though new manufacturing, transportation, and communication technologies resulted in increased product selection and reduced costs, what we as customers lost was the personal relationship with the neighborhood store owner. Service and individualized communication was not a cost-effective option for the large retail superstores and the catalog marketers. Enter the Internet.

Thanks to email, there is now a way for companies like yours to regain the ability to communicate and maintain ongoing dialogues with their customers the way they used to so many years ago. You'll be able to get to know each one individually and give them all personalized attention and service in a timely way. You'll be able to offer all your customers a nearly limitless selection of products and services and still set aside the best deals for the best customers. And you'll be able to do it all not just with a few hundred customers but with millions.

What's the secret? *Email marketing*, which we define in this book as personalized Internet direct marketing and communication based on strategic marketing program design, and data analysis. Email marketing is about helping you to understand who your most valuable customers are, establish meaningful dialogues with them, and offer them individualized service in order to realize the maximum value from them over time. It's about allowing your customers to communicate with you in ways they never could before. More broadly, email marketing is about helping you understand how you can use customer insight combined with finely targeted, personalized, and timed communication to meet your bottom-line business (and marketing) objectives.

The problem is, email marketing is still largely misunderstood and misused. What could and should be the single most effective tool for building a lasting dialogue with prospects and customers ends up not only wasting a lot of time and money but alienating customers who are sick and tired of receiving spam. It doesn't have to be this way.

AN ENGAGED CUSTOMER IS A VALUABLE CUSTOMER

Although every company will take a slightly different approach to designing a strategic email marketing program, they are all realizing how important it is to engage their customers—to have an ongoing dialogue with them, to get to know their likes and dislikes and treat them as individuals. Why? Well, let's start with a quick definition of what the word "engaged" means. Engagement is often a first formal step on the road to marriage. We can also be engaged in our work or in extracurricular activities and hobbies. Wherever or however we use the word, engagement involves some form of ongoing, active participation in a relationship. To be engaged is to be committed. To engage is to show interest and participate.

The same applies to your business. Engaged customers listen and interact with you. They care about what your company can offer them. They spend more time with you and give you a greater share of their attention. This translates into something far more tangible: a greater share of their wallet and increased long-term value. Engaged customers are also loyal; they tell their families, friends, and colleagues about you and get them engaged as well. Simply put, the more engaged your customers are, the more valuable they are.

THE NEW RULES OF ENGAGEMENT

In the old world of direct mail and telemarketing companies controlled customers' access to the information they housed in their databases. Not surprisingly, customers usually considered themselves victims, rather than beneficiaries, of direct marketing campaigns. But today customers are no longer willing to be passive targets. Increasingly, they're taking control, choosing which companies they will engage with and defining the terms of the interaction.

As a result, the old ways of dealing with customers no longer work. In the sections below we'll take a look at the *new* rules of engagement you'll have to master if you're going to successfully build loyalty and lasting relationships with your customers.

THE E-CUSTOMER EXPECTS TO BE IN CONTROL

In the Internet age, online consumers will base their decision to do business with your company as much on the intangibles as on product and price features. Customers want to communicate with a company only when *they* want to and only through the channels *they* choose. They also expect nearly unrestricted access to all sorts of information. They want you to provide direct access to your inventory database via the World Wide Web so they can see what products you have in stock and how quickly you can deliver them. New buyers expect to see what other customers are saying about whatever it is you're selling and the quality of service you provide. Today's sophisticated e-customers are also aware that the information they provide you is worth something, and they've begun to demand greater value in return for giving it up. If you don't give them what they want, there's always someone just one click away who will. The same can be said for the way business interact with each other.

This is completely unlike traditional marketing, where it's extremely difficult for individuals to control what they receive from organizations they deal with or end relationships with companies they no longer wish to hear from. In the Internet world, though, it's as easy as sending an "Unsubscribe message" (instructing the sender to remove you from his or her mailing list), setting up a spam-blocking filter (a commonly available feature in desktop mail applications enabling you to filter out unwanted or unknown email), or even opening up a new, free email account at someplace like Yahoo! or Hotmail.

Companies that recognize this shift will be in a strong position to flourish in an economy based on mass customization and individualized communication. But those who continue to rely on the old paradigms will be forced into a commodity game where the only value they can offer customers is low price, where margins become increasingly narrow and competition for customers' attention increasingly fierce and costly.

THE FOCUS OF MARKETING IS SHIFTING
FROM ACQUISITION TO RETENTION

Online marketing has come a long way since the mid-1990s. The first corporate websites were little more than digitized brochures. E-commerce pioneers such as Amazon.com, Dell, eBay, and Schwab quickly realized that the Web was about a lot more than "brochure-ware." Still, like all new businesses, they were faced with the problem of how to acquire new customers. They had to make prospects aware of the site and get them to visit it. To accomplish these goals, they began using such tools as banner advertising and affiliate programs.

But as the cost of customer acquisition skyrocketed (acquiring a single new retail customer online today can easily cost over $100), it became clear that simply generating traffic wasn't enough. To successfully run profitable online businesses, companies had to figure out how to retain existing customers and develop lasting relationships with them. Treating every customer like a first-time buyer is more than just a bad idea; it's a terrible waste of money. (In his book *The Loyalty Effect*, Frederick F. Reichheld points out that acquiring a new customer is five to ten times as expensive as selling to an existing one.) That's why today's most sophisticated marketing websites are interactive, entertaining, and informative. This enables them to keep their customers, prospects, or members engaged.

In 1998 Jupiter Communications predicted that the economic impact of retention-based marketing would exceed that of acquisition-based marketing when more than half of all Internet users became online shoppers. They predicted that this would occur in 2001—and it looks like their prediction was right on target.

INTERNET DIRECT MARKETING IS A SERVICE FUNCTION

What's going to make your customers want to come back after they've visited your website once? Why will they give you permission to contact them by email and how often will they let you do so? In short, how do you market to your customers when they control the relationships they engage in and when they can filter out or delete your messages without even reading them? The answer is quite simple: Today's customers don't want to have *marketing* relationships with the businesses they patronize; they want *service* relationships. And you develop service relationships by offering access, convenience, and value. Together, these factors make up what we call the "online service imperative." The more you focus on the online service imperative, the more your customers will want to hear from you. Developing true service relationship demands that you be comfortable handing your customers the keys to your business. The ideal service-based relationship is one in which customers depend on the company to such an extent that they become disappointed if they *don't* hear from the company.

To successfully run a business in the new customer-driven marketplace, building service-based relationships with your customers, you must orient customer communication programs around the following points:

Data Drives Relevance; Relevance Drives Engagement. If you're going to engage your customers, you have to provide them with something they find relevant. Why else would anyone listen? But if you have thousands—perhaps even millions—of customers, how can you possibly know what each one considers relevant? Through individual profiling and modeling you can get to know each and every customer, and by giving them complete access to and control of their own profiles you earn their trust and avoid violating their privacy. But remember: Every single message you send must offer something of value. And the only way to guarantee that your customers will consider you a trusted source of relevant, timely information is to make smart use of the data you collect about your customers.

Relationship Are at the Core of Sustainable Commerce. How can Amazon.com justify losing as much money as it is doing today? Why are Internet companies so highly valued with no seeming relation to such traditional economic fundamentals as revenue and profitability? A common answer to these perplexing questions is that the

Internet is in the middle of a kind of "land grab." But instead of buying actual land, companies are pouring their money into acquiring customers and establishing ongoing relationships with them. One of the keys to any successful relationship—whether it's romantic, professional, or friendly—is honest, open communication. Open communication builds solid relationships, and solid relationships allow companies to maximize the long-term value and revenue from each one.

Building Trust Is an Imperative. As organizations collect more information about their members, prospects, and customers than ever before, privacy is becoming increasingly important—and so is trust. The bottom line is that customers won't give you private information about themselves if they don't trust you. They want to control how—and with whom—that information is shared.

When current or prospective customers choose to fill out a profile and become Members of SelfCare.com (*www.selfcare.com*)—a health and wellness e-commerce site for women and their families—the first item they see is SelfCare's guarantee that all information entered will be kept private and confidential. In this way, SelfCare builds the trust necessary to ensure that a consumer looking for health information will be confident that his or her profile will not be shared with others.

Besides being intuitively the right thing to do, earning your customers' trust makes good economic sense. Once you have established a solid foundation of trust you will have a source of rich, accurate, and constantly changing information about your customers. If they trust you, they won't have any problem getting engaged with you. If they don't, they'll be very wary about giving you access to the kind of information you really need to build a lasting dialogue with them.

The Marketing Function Moves from "Telling and Selling" to "Listening and Learning." By paying close attention to what your customers tell you, you'll be better positioned to deliver true value and give your customers exactly what they want. Instead of mounting sporadic, event-driven, promotional campaigns you'll be able to provide sustained, targeted, personalized—and therefore relevant—information and offers that build customers' reliance on your brand and boost their loyalty. MyPlay (www.myplay.com) runs a service that lets you store your digital (i.e., MP3) music on the Web in a private personal storage locker. All you have to do to get one is answer a few very basic questions. Additional details are optional. As you store your music, MyPlay learns from what it sees. Every time it communicates with you by email, it asks you additional questions. And the more you use its service, the more in tune it gets with your preferences and music tastes. As the music industry evolves and it becomes possible to sell digital music over the Internet, MyPlay will be in a perfect position to capitalize on the relationships and the knowledge it has of its members' interests.

Always Ask Permission before Initiating a Dialogue. In his book *Permission Marketing*, Seth Godin introduced the concept of asking prospects or customers for permission before attempting to communicate with them. Back then, this was a completely new idea for marketing organizations that were accustomed to getting potential customers' attention by sending unsolicited mail or making phone calls. But besides that, it's simply polite to ask whether someone is interested in hearing from you before you attempt to engage them in a dialogue. In the online world, though, not asking—and getting—permission is more than just rude; it's risky business. No reputable company wants to be labeled as a spammer. Besides, while there is no federal regulation governing how companies can use customer data today, I believe that this will change in the near future—and it is never too early for your company to begin preparing.

CHANGING THE WAY YOU COMMUNICATE WITH YOUR CUSTOMERS

Besides learning the new rules of engagement, if you're going to be successful in the Internet age, you'll need to understand what's driving the change. The global network we call the Internet and the shift to digital communication have created a kind of interconnectedness that's having a huge impact on the way business is transacted in today's economy. It's an impact no company can afford to ignore. Your customers, staff, prospects, partners, vendors, and suppliers, and even your competitors, are all on the same network at the same time. They all have access to nearly the same information and they can get it 24 hours a day, in every corner of the globe. Below I outline several factors that are having a tremendous influence on communication between companies and their customers in the evolving world of e-business.

DIGITAL COMMUNICATION IS UBIQUITOUS

We live in an increasingly interconnected economy. As this book is being published, over 50 percent of U.S. households are connected to the Internet. Every computer with Internet access is connected to and can communicate with every other Internet-connected computer anywhere in the world. In addition, wireless devices such as cellular telephones, personal organizers, pagers, and even television are increasingly becoming part of this vast, global network.

As more and more communication becomes digital the boundaries between the functionality of all these devices are blurring. The Internet today supports Web pages, email, instant messaging, and basic telephony and in the not-too-distant future it will also become a primary network for video and voice communication.

TECHNICAL INNOVATION AND ADOPTION ARE DRIVING CHANGE

Technology is a critical factor driving much of the change we're experiencing in marketing and customer communications. Three pieces of technology are absolutely essential to helping companies cope with these profound changes.

The World Wide Web. With the Internet acting as the glue that ties information systems together, where your actual resources are located has become fairly irrelevant. Applications are being hosted remotely by application service providers (ASPs). And it's not at all uncommon that a company's website is hosted at one physical location, the e-commerce section and inventory management catalog at a second location, customer service at a third, and email marketing systems at a fourth.

Email. This means of communication has become ubiquitous and is used by everyone from individuals and small businesses to Fortune 500 corporations. Internet access can be had for only a few dollars a month—or for free, in some instances—and modems are now standard equipment on new computers. The only barrier to sending and receiving email is access to a computer.

Database and storage technology. Fast access to complex data sets and low-cost data storage are changing how companies think about managing customer information. Terabyte (1,000 gigabytes) databases are already commonplace and pentabyte (1,000 terabytes) databases aren't far behind.

THERE IS A GROWING INFORMATION GLUT

Consumers are constantly being bombarded with information. Hundreds of billions of dollars are spent every year trying to reach and influence the U.S. population alone. The U.S. Postal Service delivered over 230 billion pieces of mail last year and approximately 1 billion emails are sent over the Internet on an average day. Depending on the research firm we choose to believe, the average email user gets between 54 and 93 emails per week, a number that increases in direct proportion to the length of time the person has been using email. With all the information consumers are exposed to on a daily basis, it's getting harder and harder to separate the good from the bad. It all becomes so much clutter and noise after a while and people pay attention only to information from sources they recognize and have a positive relationship with.

RICH CUSTOMER DATA IS EVERYWHERE

Customer data is the foundation from which all insight into customer behavior and value is derived. Every single noncash consumer purchase, for example, is recorded electronically somewhere. This is the kind of data that allows marketers to get to know their customers, send relevant and timely communications to them, recognize them on repeat visits, and service them better each time they shop. This information is so valuable that entire industries have sprung up to collect, sort, and sell it.

With the advent of the Internet, gathering information about customers' behavior, interests, and buying patterns has been taken to an unprecedented level. Net marketers can easily compile information about almost everything users do on their websites, such as what pages they are viewing, which products they searched for and which ones they chose to find out more about, how often they visit the site, or whether they're first-time visitors. It's also very simple for consumers to fill out online forms that ask for more specific information about their likes and preferences. Best of all, almost all this information is available in real time. Leading online retailers and marketers are beginning to use the real-time data they collect and provide additional value by quickly identifying patterns in customer behavior and instantly suggesting related products or services.

THE ECONOMICS OF DIGITAL CUSTOMER DIALOGUE ARE NEW

Every communication with a customer or prospective customer has a cost associated with it. In the past, this "cost of contact" placed severe limits on the type and the amount of communicating business did.

The cost of sending a piece of mail is linked to the price of paper, printing, and postage. The cost of making an outbound telephone call is tied to telecommunications costs and to the salaries paid to the people making the calls. These per-contact costs may decrease a little with volume, but each additional contact adds something to the total bill.

On the Internet, though, the economics are different. While it may cost $3 to handle a telephone order, the cost of taking that order on the web might be $0.25 more than a tenfold decrease. With email the economics get even more extreme. At scale, incremental costs of contact are very close to zero. Of course, if person-to-person dialogue is required, the costs would be similar whether the contact is on- or offline. But compared to other media, the lower costs of online customer communication are having a profound impact on how companies interact with their customers. Overall, individual customer communication is no longer governed by the economics of contact, but rather by the economics of relationship management.

CHANGING YOUR FOCUS FROM
PRODUCT TO CUSTOMER

A potential customer shows up at your website, clicks around for a few minutes, and disappears. Getting that customer to come to your site in the first place probably cost you a lot of money, but if she leaves without telling you something about herself, chances are you've heard the last of her. You have no way to reach out and invite her back. But what if you could engage all your customers on their first visit? What if you could convince them to tell you just enough about themselves to give you a snapshot of who they are and then get their permission to contact them again? It's sort of like meeting an intriguing stranger at a party and getting her phone number.

There are two types of companies: customer-centered and product-centered. The first, not surprisingly, focuses on customers' needs and tries to offer solutions to their problems; the second focuses on product features and leaves it up to the customer to put the pieces together. If I am buying a new computer, for example, a customer-centered company would ask me what I'm planning to use the computer for and would suggest appropriate solutions. A product-centered company, though, would try to sell me on megabytes and megahertz, peripherals and software packages, without bothering to find out whether I really needed any of that.

United is a classic example of the product-centered airline company. Whenever I call to change, inquire about, or confirm my travel plans, I am asked to provide some "product information": "What flight are you on sir?" (What product have you purchased?) I usually don't know my flight number, so the operator asks for a record locator. Given that I am normally in a car, perhaps on my way to the airport, I don't often have this information handy. But I do usually know roughly when my flight is scheduled to leave and from what airport. With that information, the operator can suggest a flight number, and it's only then that she asks my name to look me up. If she finds me on the first try we're in business. I'm usually not that lucky. The situation usually goes like this:

> "How can I help you today, Mr. Brondmo?"
> "Well, I lost my luggage on my last leg and was wondering if you could put a trace on it."
> "I am very sorry, Mr. Brondmo, I can only handle your reservation. You need to call our 800 number for lost luggage. Would you like that number?"

I call the number and, after a ten-minute wait, have to repeat the whole ordeal.

United's systems are organized around flights or products, not around customers. But imagine how things would be if the moment I gave my name or frequent-flyer number they could pull up my complete record—past, present, and future.

> "Thank you for calling, Mr. Brondmo, I see you're on our 12:50 flight to JFK this afternoon. How can I help you?"
> "I need to change my return to include a stopover in Denver."
> "That's for the day after tomorrow, right? Would you like to fly the same flights you did three weeks ago and sit in the same seats?"
> "Yep."
> "Okay. You're all confirmed and we have you in an aisle seat, 10B. Is there anything else I can do for you today?"

Don Peppers and Martha Rogers, Ph.D., have been the primary force behind popularizing the concept of one-to-one marketing, as demonstrated by the above example. In their books, starting with their 1993 classic *The One-to-One Future: Building Relationships One Customer at a Time,* as well as their newsletters, speeches, and the work of their company, The Peppers and Rogers Group, they have been instrumental in helping companies become customer-focused. While the one-to-one concept is simple and sensible, it is difficult to implement. Even if one ignores the legacy problems of product- and transaction-oriented information systems, moving an organization from a product orientation to a customer orientation is a major undertaking.

If you haven't already done so, you'll need to shift your company's focus from selling your products to servicing your customers. You won't be able to succeed as an Internet marketer or engage your customers unless you do. When you go to Hewlett Packard's website to buy a computer system you don't want to have to get the printer from the printer division, the laptop from the computer division, and the printer cartridge from the cartridge division. The way HP chooses to structure its internal business should be completely transparent to you. You want a solution, not a bunch of products. And you expect HP to deal with you based on your needs and interests.

The size and scope of your organization will naturally affect how you manage your customer-centered email marketing programs. If you're a small organization with only one operating unit and one core business, you need to recognize every customer in every transaction. But if you're as big as Hewlett Packard, you may find that it's not necessary or practical to coordinate customer contact activities across all divisions. (There's not likely to be much overlap, for example, between customers in HP's Medical Equipment and Consumer Computing divisions.)

TWENTY-FIRST CENTURY MARKETING: MANAGING *RELATIONSHIP CAPITAL*

In the information economy, *information is both the ultimate commodity and the ultimate asset,* and whoever has access to the best, the richest, and the most accurate information has the strongest competitive advantage. The most valuable information of all is the information that merchants and service providers have about their customers. If you know who your customers are, what they do, what they like, and what they want, you can offer them products best suited to meet their needs. You can deliver highly personalized service that will enable you to realize the maximum value from the relationships you establish with each and every one of your customers.

In fact, a new paradigm is to view the marketer as an asset manager. Twenty-first-century marketers manage their customers' personal information in much the same way that a bank or investment firm manages financial assets. In the online world, customers are rapidly learning to entrust marketers with this valuable asset only if they feel confident that they will give them some tangible value in return, and only as long as they know that they can withdraw it at any time. Just like the customers in a financial institution, online customers will naturally choose to engage with the "information managers" who generate the highest return on their assets.

The way that the marketer generates such a "return" on the personal information under management for a customer is by building and managing customer relationships. Let's collectively refer to these information and relationship assets as *relationship capital*. Traditionally, organizations have several forms of capital under management: financial capital, human capital, intellectual capital, and—of increasing importance—relationship capital. *The goal of the twenty-first-century marketer is to maximize the long-term return on an organization's relationship capital.*

So how does this work? Harlequin Enterprises (www.eHarlequin.com), which publishes more books than any other publisher in the world, decided to use email to communicate with its readers. Harlequin's online customers—mostly college-educated professional women—are extremely loyal, making one or more purchases every month. As a special service to them, Harlequin created the *eHarlequin* newsletter program, a special email newsletter program that enables readers to get book announcements, romantic tips, recipes for romantic meals, and check their horoscopes for a glimpse into their romantic fortunes. Harlequin's email marketing program is highly individualized and subscribers can sign up for topics such as "Men in Uniform," "Paranormal Romance," "Amnesiacs," and "The Bodyguard." They can also elect to be notified when their favorite authors publish new books.

Harlequin is acting like a customer information manager, carefully gathering and managing customer data on its customers' interests and preferences, and in turn providing a service that informs, amuses, educates, and entertains. The company is also engaging its most valuable and loyal customers in an ongoing dialogue. Harlequin doesn't have to use promotional gimmicks to solicit input and feedback from customers. Instead, it willingly shares information because it knows it'll receive something of value in return. The marketers at Harlequin are generating a significant return to the customers and to the company on its relationship capital.

Engaging your customers in dialogue isn't something you can leave to chance—it's an absolute imperative if your business is to survive. As the euphoria of Internet retail has begun to wear off, companies can no longer count on Wall Street to give them carte blanche to lose money. Sure, it still makes good business sense to invest heavily in operations in order to accelerate growth, but sound business fundamentals have begun to matter again: Company models need to include a break-even projection. And when fundamentals matter, nothing is more important than having loyal customers. In the next chapter we'll look at the incredible power of email as a direct marketing medium. When email and direct marketing are combined to create Internet direct marketing, you can service your customers in ways never before possible. You can stay in touch with them on a regular basis, inform and entertain them, encourage and listen to their feedback. In short, you can engage them.

CHAPTER 2

EMAIL AND MARKETING:
A MATCH MADE IN HEAVEN

EMAIL IS THE MOST powerful direct marketing tool that has ever existed. So when it comes to Internet marketing, the question isn't *whether* email should be a part of the landscape, but *how* to use it as a sustainable tool to serve marketers and consumers alike.

Current email direct marketing efforts are meeting with great success. People generally open, read, and respond to their email—especially when it comes from a company they know and do business with. The best email marketing programs, in fact, routinely enjoy response rates above 30 percent, while even fairly simple promotional marketing campaigns routinely see a 4 to 6 percent response (compared to the average 1 to 2 percent response rate from traditional direct mail campaigns).

There are signs, though, that the honeymoon may be coming to an end. According to eMarketer, a research firm specializing in Internet marketing, the average active Internet-connected computer user receives 97 emails per week. And as people become more and more inundated they get increasingly likely to delete marketing and promotional email before they even open it, let alone consider the included offers. Some people are even creating filters or subscribing to spam protection services that block certain kinds of email altogether. Your greatest challenge, then, as you do business online is to rise above the clutter, to figure out what's going to make a customer or prospect pay attention to your email communication.

OUT WITH THE OLD AND IN WITH THE NEW

Traditional off-line direct-response marketing is a $160 billion-a-year industry, accounting for 60 percent of total marketing and advertising spending. Many of the practices and much of the experience from this industry continue to be very valuable as companies move their direct marketing online. At the same time, there are a number of significant differences among the ways marketing is conducted offline and online, as the following table illustrates.

Traditional Direct Marketing	Internet Direct Marketing
Campaigns	Programs and relationships
Lists	Integrated customer databases
Broadcast monologue	Interactive dialogue
Groups and segments	Individuals
Intermittent contact	Sustained contact
Promotional	Informational, educational, entertaining, and promotional
Involuntary (opt-out)	Voluntary (opt-in)

Be mindful that these differences are not just changes in language and semantics. They represent a fundamental shift in the way you will use the Internet to engage your customers. "Old world" terminology such as *campaign* and *list* are used to describe discrete events while words such as *program* and *customer database* imply continuous, ongoing communication. And while *promotional* contact is the focus of most traditional direct marketing, the new technologies and the new economics of Internet direct marketing make it possible for the first time ever to create a blended contact mix of *informational, educational, entertaining* and *promotional* communications.

TYPES OF EMAIL MARKETING PROGRAMS

Spam	**Campaigns and opt-in lists**	**Customer dialogue and service**
• Unsolicited	• One to many	• Individualized
• Unexpected	• One message	• Integrated
• Unwanted	• One way	• Interactive
• Soon-to-be unlawful	• Exclusively promotional	• Informational
	• List driven	• Program-oriented
		• Profile- and data-driven

From spam to customer dialogue and service.

Use the new language of Internet direct marketing when you describe and design your programs and you will find that it influences the very program itself.

THE EMAIL MARKETING CONTINUUM

The phrase "email marketing" describes a large number of programs that incorporate email and some function of marketing or customer communication. At one end of the spectrum we have spam. At the other end we have customer dialogue and service.

When a new medium is first invented, the natural inclination is to use it to do what was done before, but more efficiently. Film was first seen as a cost-effective way to distribute stage plays, and the first television broadcasts were simply recordings of popular radio shows such as *Amos and Andy*. Yet film developed to become its own medium with its own language and conventions that are very different from theater, and television today is nothing like radio. In much the same way, people saw the Internet in its early days as little more than a cheaper, faster way of executing direct marketing campaigns. It hasn't taken long to figure out that the Internet is fundamentally different from other marketing media. Nevertheless, too many people still consider Internet direct marketing to be an extension of traditional direct marketing. Let's take a look at why using email and the Internet this way misses the point entirely.

SPAM

While traditional direct mailers normally collect or purchase lists of names and addresses for the purpose of contacting prospective customers, that practice is very much frowned upon on the Internet. Most people consider unsolicited email an invasion of privacy. But considering how easy it is to delete spam from an email box—a couple of clicks and it's in the virtual trash—it's quite surprising how intensely most of us react to spam.

Although we tolerate the junk circulars in our mailboxes and the steady barrage of commercials on the radio and network television, most of us deeply resent telemarketing, advertising in movie theaters or on cable TV, and unsolicited email. The reason seems obvious: Radio, television, and junk mail come to us "for free"—that is, the direct costs are borne by the sender—whereas we pay for access to the Internet, movie theaters, cable TV, and home telephones out of our own pockets. And, we feel, this gives us the right to control who contacts us and what we listen to.

Virtually every Internet service provider from AOL to the smallest ISP has a zero tolerance policy and is very sensitive to marketers who do not adhere to the Internet's established rules and conventions. Still, many experts now estimate that about 10 percent of all email is spam. It's become such a problem that the state of California has actually tried to control it by requiring that unsolicited email be clearly labeled in the message header as advertising. Yet enforcement can be difficult. It is possible for an ISP to block email from a known spammer, but only when the address used by the spammer to send unsolicited mail is known. As a result, we are witnessing an ongoing game of "cat and mouse," with clever measures and countermeasures constantly being devised in the spam wars.

Being labeled a spammer can seriously damage a company's brand image. For this reason, reputable businesses that have ventured into this territory, accidentally or by design, have quickly retreated. Early in its existence, for example, Amazon.com sent out an unsolicited mailing to thousands of its customers. Within days, angry customers had forwarded copies of the email to the media. Articles showed up in the press headlined "Spamazon.com." Needless to say, Amazon.com put a quick end to that marketing program and issued a public statement about its new email and privacy policies.

If spam is so annoying and ineffective, why does it still exist? Because it's so cheap to blast out large volumes of email that even the smallest response and conversation rates can make it economically feasible.

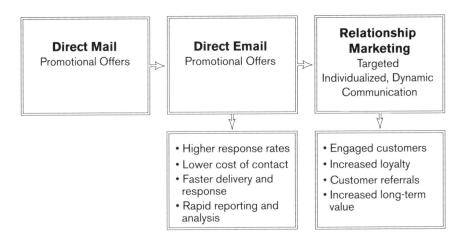

The evolution of email marketing.

DIRECT EMAIL—FASTER, BETTER, CHEAPER DIRECT MAIL

Direct email is built on the relatively new Internet concept of "opt-in," which ensures that the recipients of an email campaign have given the marketer permission to contact them.

In the early days of e-commerce, most email marketing programs were based on the tried-and-true principles of direct mail. Every email was intended to generate a purchase and the success of a direct email program was—and for the most part still is—measured by the return on investment (ROI) for each individual campaign. As we might expect, this approach has been quite successful in the online world. Compared to their offline counterparts, direct email campaigns are better (response rates have generally been significantly higher than offline), cheaper (sending email is a lot less expensive than printing and mailing snail mail), and faster (turnaround on direct email campaigns is measured in days, not in the weeks or months of traditional offline campaigns).

Despite these benefits, direct email isn't particularly effective for anything other than one-way, promotion-oriented mailings. It hasn't taken full advantage of the Internet's unique characteristics. What if a customer visits a site he likes but isn't quite ready to buy anything—how can he let the company know he'd like them to keep him up to date on certain products or information? Or what if the customer makes a purchase now and then—but only if she receives frequent information in the form of articles and product reviews tailored to her interests? How can the company notify customers when something they might be interested in becomes available?

RELATIONSHIP MARKETING—REACHING
THE POTENTIAL OF THE NEW MEDIUM

Although direct email is a better, faster, and cheaper version of direct mail, you can reach the true potential of the Internet only if you focus your efforts on managing customer relationships, not individual marketing campaigns. When designing a marketing program grounded in relationship marketing principles, we are no longer looking to optimize the economic value of every individual email campaign. As a matter of fact, we don't even talk about campaigns at all; we talk about ongoing programs. Our goal, therefore, is to maximize each customer's value over time by building long-term relationships and loyalty. As a result, not every contact needs to be promotional. In fact, it shouldn't be. We can send a customer email messages containing highly personalized information, educational material, and content meant purely to entertain and amuse. As we discussed in Chapter 1, the new economics of the Internet enables us to build these kinds of programs because "cost of contact" is no longer a relevant metric. Marketing costs move from individual contacts (each email sent costs money) to customers under management (managing each customer relationship, regardless of how often you contact them, costs money). The cost moves from promotional campaigns to service and "publishing," which are essential to building loyalty and lasting relationships.

FROM A LIST PARADIGM TO A
LIVE CUSTOMER PROFILE PARADIGM

Traditional direct marketing is based on campaigns and lists. Lists support campaigns, which are one-time mailings. An important step in every campaign, is list selection, which helps marketers target their campaigns using such criteria as purchase history, customer value, demographics, etc. A number of service providers specialize in performing list-related functions such as "list hygiene": merging and purging lists, enhancing them with third-party data, and, most important, "deduping" them—weeding out duplicate listings of individuals. List hygiene helps companies avoid costly multiple mailings to the same address or mailings to invalid addresses. Keeping lists current can be difficult and messy tasks. And so is correlating results of a campaign to the list that was used for the mailing. Both these functions are essential, though, not only to track the return on investment of each campaign but to improve the quality of the list for future mailings.

Using lists in this way may work fairly well for traditional, campaign-style marketing or direct mail, but it is highly inefficient as we move to more sophisticated relationship marketing programs. The world of real-time, data-driven email marketing is built around "live profiles." Live profiles, which form the basis for continuous marketing programs, are stored in a database and constantly updated. They can be examined and modified at any time by the customer or the company. In Chapter 5, we take a look at developing a customer model, which is the abstract basis for a live customer profile.

This isn't to say that lists are never used in email marketing. There are, in fact, occasions when lists come in handy. We'll talk about some of them later in the book.

SO WHAT'S SO GREAT ABOUT EMAIL?

IT'S PROACTIVE AND OUTBOUND

Websites, by their very nature, are passive: they have to wait for visitors to come to them. And most people regularly visit only a few sites. Email, however, allows you to change this dynamic by reaching out and delivering information. You can reach people who may have an occasional interest in your website but who wouldn't visit it very often, as well as to contact regular customers to encourage them to visit—and buy—again.

Consider iOwn, an online home mortgage broker that runs a mortgage rate watch service. All you need to do is provide iOwn with your email address and the interest rate and type of loan you are looking for and the company will notify you by email daily, either with the day's rate or only when a specific rate is met. For someone looking to purchase or refinance a home, this is a very useful and timely service. For iOwn, it's a powerful, proactive marketing program that gives it a good reason to stay in touch with its prospective customers.

IT'S TIMELY

While traditional direct marketing is a slow process, email is a real-time medium. Members, prospects, and customers can be notified by email within seconds of an event occurring. For example,

E*TRADE® notifies customers when the stocks they are following go above or below certain stated limits. One natural health products company sends reminders to its customers a week before their vitamin supply is due to run out. As these examples demonstrate direct marketing on the Internet may require that you make some major technological and organizational changes. Your systems must be able to collect, analyze, and report data in real time as well as run continuous email programs. And your entire marketing organization must be prepared to design and implement campaigns and programs that generate immediate responses and require instant follow-up.

IT'S PERSONAL

My email box is different from anyone else's in the world, meaning that you and I won't ever receive the exact same mix of emails. The messages we all receive are determined by who we know, where we work, and who we've given our email address to. Friends and family send each other personal emails. Companies broadcast announcements to their employees by email. Professional colleagues send each other messages and memos by email. And businesses can build relationships with their customers by sending personalized email.

IT'S COST-EFFECTIVE

Email costs a fraction of regular mail and telephone calls—and it's normally a lot more convenient for the person on the receiving end. But while mail and telephones are ubiquitous, just over half of the U.S. population currently uses email, and most established businesses may have email addresses for only a small percentage of their customers. One leading white goods manufacturer has the names of over 35 million customers in its worldwide customer database—but fewer than 1 million customer email addresses. By increasing its database of email addresses, the company will be able to cut its customer communications costs substantially while increasing its opportunity to establish more frequent, personalized and relevant contact.

As we discussed in Chapter 1, in traditional direct marketing the fixed costs of developing a campaign are small relative to the variable costs involved in making the actual contact—paper, printing, postage, and so forth. On the Internet the economics are different. The fixed costs of setting up an email marketing program are comparable to offline, but the variable costs are significantly lower, incrementally approaching zero at scale. In short, it costs nearly the same to make 10,000 contacts, or 100,000.

IT'S MEASURABLE

Thanks to current technology, you can measure and track response activity and get a clear insight into what works and what doesn't. You can monitor who received which emails, who opened them, who responded by clicking on which links, how long it took to respond, and whether they made a purchase after clicking through to a website. If you pay attention to all this data, you'll have a tremendous opportunity to refine your programs and improve the relevance and service levels your emails provide.

SIX MYTHS ABOUT EMAIL MARKETING

Despite all these advantages, some people still doubt that email can be used to create the sort of personal dialogue we've been discussing. "It's all just spam," they say. "What makes you think people are going to want to receive your emails?" To a large extent, their doubt—and their corresponding lack of success in implementing a successful email marketing program—is driven by six common myths about email marketing. Let's take a quick look at each of these myths.

MYTH 1: ASKING PEOPLE WHAT THEY WANT NEVER WORKS

In the offline world of direct marketing, asking people to fill out forms expressing their preferences is not particularly effective. Though it may be a useful means of collecting general information, it's common knowledge that surveys aren't a very good indicator of individual customer value. To start with, you'll probably have to offer incentives and prizes to get people to fill out the forms in the first place. Many fill out the forms for no other reason than to have a shot at the prize, and instead of the truth, they write down answers they think will help them win. People like these don't have a lot of future value as prospective customers.

Furthermore, it's nearly impossible to use the information to customize marketing to each individual: it would simply cost too much. Yet another problem is that customers have no way to change the information they give you at a later time. When filling out paper forms people have no idea where the information is ending up, what it will be used for, and, most important, what they'll get in return.

On the Internet, however, asking people what they want really works. This is because you can deliver real, immediate, and tangible value to each of your customers based on what they tell you. The online service imperative tells us that when people use the sign-up process as the beginning of a service relationship, they willingly share and update their personal information. If you tell them why you are asking for information, make filling in everything but the essentials optional, tie their answers directly to some kind of service and value, and make your privacy statement easy to access and to understand, they'll engage. If you make it clear to people who fill out the forms that they are in control and can come back and remove their names from the program or change or update their answers at any time, your customers will enter into an ongoing dialogue with you instead of simply answering questions on a one-time survey.

MYTH 2: I HAVE ONLY ONE CHANCE TO ASK MY CUSTOMERS QUESTIONS

When designing a customer sign-up process, marketers often fear that if they don't ask a whole bunch of questions right away, they'll never have another opportunity. "It's really hard to get a customer to come back and answer more questions," they say. Sure, some customers and prospects won't come back and engage with you more than once, so unless you ask all your questions up front, you won't be able to capture all the information you need to understand their interests. But how important is it to get these people to sign up in the first place? According to the online service imperative, your customers will return and engage further if you provide them with value. If they don't come back, it's because you're not meeting their needs or they're no longer interested in what you have to offer. The beauty of the Internet is how simple it is to ask people questions on an ongoing basis. You can drop in a question or two every time they visit your website, and you can ask questions right in your emails. Asking someone to fill out your three-page survey on a first encounter is no way to begin a relationship. That may have worked in the past, but it sure doesn't on the Internet.

MYTH 3: MY CUSTOMERS WON'T WANT MY EMAIL

Although it's certainly true that the last thing most people want is more email, your customers really do want to hear from you. Maybe not every day or every week—perhaps even once a month would be too much—but if you've got something interesting and informative to say or something fun and exciting to sell, your customers will want to know. Your challenge, then, is to figure out what they'd be interested in hearing about. If the answer is "nothing," you've got bigger problems than this book can address.

MYTH 4: EMAIL MARKETING IS EASY

It's pretty easy to send somebody you know a nice, personal letter, and even easier to send a nice personal email. It takes a bit more work, though, to send personal emails to ten people and a lot more to send them to hundreds (or thousands or millions) of people—especially if you're trying to make each communication relevant and interesting enough to get the recipient to visit your website or buy something. Throw in trying to keep track of how people respond to each letter, following up, and maintaining a dialogue beyond the first contact, and you've got a problem that can be solved only through advanced automation and strategic planning.

MYTH 5: EMAIL IS FREE

Most companies today provide free email to employees, enabling them to send and receive email from their offices and, often, from their homes or while they're on the road. The problem is that too many companies assume they can use the employee email system to manage an email marketing program. Broadcasting a small number of emails is somewhat complicated but manageable enough that you can probably do it on your existing infrastructure and server software. But even a relatively simple, continuous email marketing program requires complex technology and marketing expertise as well as ongoing marketing services and operational support and, finally, a robust IT (information technology) infrastructure—none of which are cheap.

MYTH 6: INFORMATION TECHNOLOGY WILL JUST INSTALL SOME SOFTWARE TO RUN OUR EMAIL MARKETING PROGRAMS

Some organizations consider the question of whether to make or buy their email marketing solution as a purely IT function. But it's not that easy. In a few years it may be possible to purchase off-the-shelf software that will solve organizations' more basic email marketing and customer communication needs. But the industry isn't nearly this sophisticated yet, and even if it were, each company's unique needs would require significant amounts of customization. The truth is that building an email marketing service is more of a marketing solution than an IT one. Nevertheless, any sophisticated email direct marketing program will need active support from IT.

Sadly, believing these myths has kept far too many companies from realizing email's true potential. But understanding what email can do for your business isn't enough. Even those who *do* appreciate email's power can do themselves serious harm by misusing it. The solution is to rethink the way you market your products and services—not only online, but offline as well. But as anyone who has ever been involved in trying to restructure the way an organization thinks will tell you, that's easier said than done. Your enemy is the kind of short-term, tactical thinking that fails to recognize that the Internet has fundamentally changed the way we do business. Throughout the rest of this book we'll be taking a look at the big—

and small—steps you can take to ensure that you're engaging your customers in a lasting dialogue, not just bombarding them with broadcast messages. In the next section, I'll focus on how important it is to think strategically when designing your Internet direct marketing programs. Only by taking a carefully planned, strategic approach will your company be able to fully realize email's potential as a marketing and communications tool.

PART II

TAKING
A STRATEGIC
APPROACH

CHAPTER 3

THE MANY USES OF EMAIL

A S WE'VE SEEN, the Internet is already transforming the direct marketing industry and has the potential to transform your business's approach to marketing. But no matter how much your marketing department changes, your fundamental business goals will remain constant: you still need to make people aware of your products or services, convert prospects into new customers, retain the ones who buy and turn them into loyal, long-term customers. Before we get into the specifics of designing and implementing your own program, you need to understand the broad range that email marketing covers, from acquisition campaigns to conversion programs and from retention and loyalty programs to brand-building programs. These programs exist wherever and whenever your organization— whether it's large or small, business to business (B2B) or business to consumer (B2C)—needs to establish communication with specific individuals (as opposed to departments or job functions).

EMAIL ACQUISITION PROGRAMS: MAKING A GOOD FIRST IMPRESSION

Think about your online acquisition programs as a series of forays into the dating world. Once you decide you want to start going out, you have to figure out how you're going to meet people. Will your friends set you up or will you use a matchmaking service? Will you just stop someone on the street or is there someone you know who is interested in having a relationship? Regardless of how you actually meet, there's a great deal of truth in the old saying that you only get one chance to make a first impression. The first time your company communicates with a potential member or customer is the first opportunity you have to establish your brand image in the customer's mind. Are you going to be pushy and loud or demure and shy? Are you going to be a listener or will you simply tell and sell? The tone and approach of your initial communication will determine who chooses to engage with you and on what grounds. And as we've discussed, the online service imperative says that your communication will be most effective if you make it clear up front that you are going to offer a high degree of relevance and service if the customer chooses to engage with you further. Below are the most commonly used types of acquisition programs.

OPT-IN LISTS: WHERE PERMISSION EMAIL MARKETING STARTS

The term "opt-in list" comes up a lot in discussions of e-marketing. There are really only two basic types of opt-in lists:

- *Outside lists* are operated by permission email marketing companies such as YesMail and Netcreations that sell access to the email addresses on that list. Consumers input their interests and sign up to receive relevant promotions. Although these lists are pretty pricey, they can be effective customer acquisition tools if they're operated and maintained properly. Yahoo's Yahoo! Delivers service is another example of a high-quality opt-in email list. The people on the list are Yahoo! members who've signed up to receive email about specific topics they're interested in.
- *House lists* are companies' internally generated lists of prospects and customers. ("House list" is a traditional direct marketing term for customer or prospect database. While I don't use the term house list much in this book, you will often hear people using it interchangeably with customer database.)

The one thing that both types of opt-in lists have in common is that the people on them have all given their explicit permission to be contacted by email. The quality of these lists varies, of course, depending on the amount of information known about the people on them.

When building your customer or prospect database (i.e., your house list), you need to carefully consider what you plan to do with all the email addresses you're collecting. On the one hand you might want to build your own database of prospects and customers and build long-term relationships with them. On the other hand you might want to make some money selling access to the same people. Don't try to have your cake and eat it too. A customer-oriented company focused on building long-term relationships will never sell access to its opt-in lists unless the people on it have specifically agreed to have their information shared with other companies. (See "Referral-Based Email Marketing Programs," below.) Selling access to your customer database may give you some short-term economic gain, but it's not the best way to maximize the value of the relationships you've built with your customers.

One common problem with opt-in lists is that people are usually presented with the choice to opt in or opt out at the very beginning of their relationship with the company, and they cannot or are not encouraged to interact any further. As a result, the lists often don't contain very much detail about the people on them. Because the profiles aren't rich, everyone on a given list gets the same email, which means that it can't be all that relevant for every recipient.

It is critical for the success of your program that you make it easy for your customers to engage with you by providing you with more personal information as their confidence and trust increases. So remember to design your opt-in email programs in a way that makes it possible to gather more information over time.

When building your own customer database consider the difference between using opt-in and opt-out.

- *Opt-in* means that a person must take an explicit action to receive your email, perhaps by responding to a statement on a web sign-up page or during "check out" such as: "To receive periodic email with special offers and information, please check this box." Unless people deliberately check the box, they are not signed up and will *not* receive any email.

- *Double opt-in* is, as the name implies, a stronger version of opt-in. People who check the box receive an email follow-up asking them to confirm. They must then either respond to the email or click through to a web page and restate their participation by clicking an "I accept" button on the site. Some privacy organizations are advocating double opt-in as the recommended way to assure that people are fully aware that they have just signed up for something. A more common approach is to combine opt-in with a follow-up welcome email that clearly states what the recipient has signed up for and that makes it very simple to unsubscribe in case there's been an error or a change of heart.
- *Opt-out* is the opposite of opt-in. The box on a web page would already be checked and the statement might read: "We occasionally send email with special offers and information. Please uncheck this box if you do *not* wish to receive these emails." The obvious disadvantage of opt-out is that customers must actively disengage. They might easily overlook the opt-out check box and end up participating in a program and receiving emails that they have no interest in.

Not surprisingly, opt-outs generate higher sign-up rates than opt-ins. With opt-in, however, you end up with a higher-quality list because the people who sign up do so by making an explicit choice. Going with the opt-in also reduces the chance that someone will accidentally fail to uncheck the box and later accuse you of sending spam. The option you choose will depend on what you're offering your customers and on your overall company policies on privacy and information capture.

REFERRAL-BASED EMAIL MARKETING PROGRAMS

On the Internet, word of mouth has become "word of mouse": News, gossip, slander, information, jokes, and hot new ideas all spread like wildfire. Referral-based marketing attempts to channel some of the Internet's word-spreading capabilities by allowing information to spread in a rapid but controlled manner. There are two categories of referral-based email marketing programs.

Company-Refer-a-Company Programs. CDNOW, the online music retailer (www.CDNOW.com), might recommend a DVD/CD player from Sony or promote a special offer from Ticketmaster on Bruce Springsteen concert tickets to customers who live near where he'll be performing. What CDNOW actually does is to refer its own customers to Sony or to Ticketmaster. Although this can be an effective way for companies to cross-leverage their customer databases, these types of programs can have some pitfalls. Before referring customers to other companies, businesses need to keep in mind each customer's opt-in status. What, exactly, did the customer opt-in to receive? What was the context under which he or she gave permission to be sent emails?

At eBags, an online store for bags, luggage, handbags, and accesories, (www.eBags.com), site visitors, promotion participants, and customers are invited to opt-in to the My eBags membership program. Over 90 percent of customers choose to join the My eBags program because members always receive free shipping on every order—a significant value delivered at the very outset of their eBags relationship. Program members are given the choice to also receive advance notice of sales, special offers, product previews, and updates, as well as industry news, trends, and tips within three types of email message (Special Offers & Promotions, Monthly Newsletters, and Monthly Events & Holiday Reminders). Members also receive exclusive offers from eBags marketing partners. Saying "Yes" to a My eBags email message grants the company permission to deliver to you an offer from, say, United, within the Special Offers & Promotions email you opted-in to receive. Or if you just bought a backpack for your school-age child, eBags might deliver to you a special offer on back-to-school supplies from a partner. In another variation, eBags ran a "Pack to School"™ tie-in promotion with CDNOW. All customers who made a purchase and joined the My eBags program during the promotional period received a $15 gift certificate good for a free CD. In a recent survey sent to its My eBags members, eBags determined that members enjoy receiving these offers from eBags marketing partners. However, the eBags marketing department needs to constantly ask itself whether the added value associated with delivering an exclusive offer to its My eBags members from its marketing partners is actually helping to build its core business: selling bags and accessories for all lifestyles. Would sending another added-value offer to buy flowers, test-drive a Ford Explorer, or sign up for a new long-distance carrier suppress members' response levels to buy another bag or accessory from eBags?

Friend-Tell-a-Friend Programs. On the Internet word of mouth is a mass medium. Companies realize that their own customers can be valuable sources of referrals, telling their friends, families, or colleagues about a service, special offer, or promotion they've discovered. The simplest tell-a-friend programs encourage email recipients to forward an email to others they think may be interested. The email will contain a call to action—most commonly a link—encouraging the recipient to do or buy something. More sophisticated tell-a-friend programs such as the one run by Petopia (www.petopia.com) ask customers to enter the email addresses of their friends and associates in a web form. This automatically delivers an email invitation to these prospective customers. Such an invitation might look like this:

> *Dear Joe:*
> *Your friend Brett asked us to send you this email to tell you about an exciting new service that she has signed up for . . .*

Having Brett give you her boyfriend Joe's email address is better than encouraging her to forward an email to him because having Joe's email address helps you keep track of how well your referral programs are working. You can monitor exactly how many customers tell their friends and how many new customers you get as a result. It also enables you to offer incentives to Brett ("Sign up ten people and get a $50 gift certificate at your favorite online store") and track the results. Tell-a-friend programs typically generate very high quality leads and are often referred to as "viral" because the news about a new product or service spreads from person to person like a virus.

BANNERS AND EMAIL

As part of a program dubbed Weboutfitter, Intel has been running a banner advertising campaign designed to encourage computer owners to sign up for updates and information about products that make the best use of their processor. Users who click on the banner are taken to a web form and asked to provide an email address and first name as well as to answer a few short questions about their interests and needs. The goal of the program is to continue to link the Intel brand with good service. The message is clear: Sign up and Intel will keep you informed of the latest developments and ensure that you get the maximum benefit from your powerful computer.

SWEEPSTAKES

A banner advertisement or promotional link on a website might announce a prize to be given away to the winner of a particular drawing. Clicking on the link brings up an entry form requesting an email address and perhaps asking a few questions. If the company's goal is to later send entrants nonsweepstakes-related emails, the entry form must contain an explicit opt-in (or opt-out) question.

ShopperConnecton Inc., (www.shopperconnection.com) is a consortium of top-tier e-retailers (based on service and product quality) that has created co-marketing and cross-promotional activities that reduce customer acquisition costs. One such program is a bimonthly newsletter that advertises each member's promotions and savings. To develop its email marketing database for this newsletter, ShopperConnection ran a "Win a $25,000 Shopping Spree" sweepstakes promotion. Entrants were asked to fill in the contest entry and indicate whether they would like to become a ShopperConnection member and receive the newsletter. Becoming a member automatically subscribed the entrant to every company participating in the consortium. Members then received a newsletter with promotions from all 15 retailers. The recipients could, of course, modify the contents of the newsletter by unsubscribing from specific retailers right in the email.

The biggest problem with using sweepstakes and other similar types of promotions for customer acquisition is that there is a disconnect between what people sign up for (an opportunity to win the $25,000 shopping spree) and your objectives as a marketer (converting the person who signed up into a loyal customer). As a result, sweepstakes-based promotions have among the lowest conversion rates in the business.

HOW MUCH WILL IT COST?

One of the most important factors you'll need to consider when running any of the programs we discussed above is how much it will cost you to acquire each lead. Let's imagine that you're planning to run a $10,000 sweepstakes program that will use banners to drive people to a simple sign-up form designed to get people to answer two basic questions and provide an email address. Your cost breakdown might look like this:

Program planning and management	$2,500
Banner and sign-up form design/development	4,000
Media buy: 500,000 impressions @$20 CPM	10,000
Database operation and maintenance	5,000
Contest administration	2,000
Contest giveaway	10,000
Total sweepstakes cost	$33,500

If your campaign generates 500,000 banner impressions resulting in 25,000 entering the contest (a 5 percent sign-up rate), the cost per entrant is $1.34. The problem with this calculation is that it doesn't take into consideration how qualified each participant is as a prospective customer. This, naturally, will have a significant impact on your cost to convert participants into customers. You might, for example, have to run more email campaigns to identify actual qualified prospects from the sweepstakes. The costs of these additional campaigns and the resulting conversion rates will yield the actual customer acquisition cost for the sweepstakes. The cost of running these additional email campaigns might be something like this:

Program planning and management	$1,000
Email campaign design and development	500
Email campaign execution and tracking	5,000
Total email conversion campaign cost	$6,500

Assuming that the follow-on email campaigns end up generating a (high) industry average of 0.4 percent total conversion to purchase, of your 25,000 contest entrants, 100 will actually buy something. This means that the cost of acquiring each new customer is $400 ($33, 500 + $6,500 = $40,000 / 100 = $400). According to the 1999 "State of Online Retailing" study conducted by Boston Consulting Group, the average online customer acquisition cost for pure play online retailers in 1998 was $42. Although this cost has been increasing rapidly since the BCG study, our $400 cost is clearly far too high, and we would probably not continue our sweepstakes program.

There are a number of factors that may directly impact your acquisition costs in this scenario. Clearly, the better qualified your sweepstakes entrants are and the more targeted and personalized you make your follow-up emails, the higher your response rate will be. As your response rate rises, your conversion rates probably will too. If you could double the conversion rate to 0.8 percent you would decrease your acquisition cost to $200 per customer. That's still above the industry average, but its a lot better than $400.

CONVERSION PROGRAMS: GOING STEADY

Let's continue with the analogy of dating relationships. If your date is someone you're thinking you could potentially have a long-term relationship with (and the feeling is mutual), you'll probably have gotten a phone number along with permission to make contact again. Similarly, once you've done your customer acquisition work, you'll have the email addresses of a group of people who have given you permission to contact them again. If you were paying close enough attention during your first "date" with your prospective customers, you'll know what their interests are. Sending them an email demonstrating that will make them feel appreciated and keep them interested in maintaining a dialogue with you.

Just as your goal might be to convince your date to go steady with you, your goal in email marketing is to convince your customers to have an exclusive relationship with you. As people sign up at your website, enter a sweepstakes, or identify themselves in some way, it is the goal of your conversion program to guide them along the path to making a purchase or using your services.

Going back to our hypothetical example, the first step in a conversion program is to qualify the sweepstakes entrants as leads. Once you have a base of qualified leads, you can move to trying to convert them. But it's important to know when to give up. In our example, for instance, 25,000 people entered your contest, but only a small percentage of them will end up staying with you for the long haul. Most are simply interested in the possibility of winning something. So after several unsuccessful attempts to convert a lead, it's normally a good idea to break off communication—just as you might do with someone who stopped returning your phone calls.

CareGuide (www.careguide.com), the online elder- and childcare solution provider, is building its business around a complex, "sequenced" conversion process. CareGuide knows that it takes more than a single contact—email or otherwise—to help people fully understand the care-giving process and make the best decision for their loved ones. CareGuide's goal is to send a sequence of emails personalized to the specific care situation and needs of the caregivers and carefully timed to lead them through the decision-making process.

To see how this might work, imagine that you've visited the CareGuide website and filled out a short form with a few questions about your care needs and told CareGuide that, in your case, you need help in locating the right care providers in your area for your parent's situation. Over the course of the next few days, CareGuide transmits a series of emails that guide you through the process of finding care providers, from understanding the available care options to understanding which option is best for you. As you learn,

CareGuide points you back from the email to specific tools on the website that help you connect with several home-care providers that meet your needs. With your permission, CareGuide transfers the direct relationship to the actual care provider and takes itself out of the loop. To add the final touches to this conversion process, you may receive an email again from CareGuide two weeks later to see that everything is going well and asking whether there's anything else it can assist you with. It may also ask for feedback on the process and the service it provided.

Most important, since your care situation is continually changing, in every email CareGuide also reinforces the value of returning to the site to update the information about your situation so it can continue to send you email "curriculum" to help you through the next phase in the care-giving process, which could be about how you finance the care needed, how to handle legal issues, and so on.

EMAIL RETENTION PROGRAMS: MAKING A COMMITMENT

Ironically, at this point, after having acquired leads and converted some of them into customers, most businesses will probably lose money making this first sale. The majority of businesses make a profit only when their customers come back and make additional purchases or when the business can convince customers and members to use their website or service on an ongoing basis. When a customer buys from you once, there's a better chance that he or she will buy again than that a completely new prospect will buy for the first time. That's exactly why retaining existing customers is one of the most important goals of email marketing.

Imagine that you're running a single campaign to send a targeted, personalized promotion to 200,000 existing customers. The cost breakdown might be the same as it was in the sweepstakes example.

Campaign planning and management	$1,000
Email campaign design and development	500
Email campaign execution and tracking	5,000
Total email up-sell campaign cost	$6,500

In this case, however, let's make the conservative assumption that the email generates a 5 percent click-through (response) rate and a conversion of click-through to purchase of about 10 percent, which puts conversion at 0.5 percent of total recipients. So, of the 200,000 who receive your email, 10,000 (5 percent) will click through and 1,000 (10 percent of 10,000) will actually buy something. Thus, the cost of selling to an existing customer is $6.50 ($6,500 / 1,000), or approximately one-seventh the $42.00 average cost to e-retailers of acquiring a new customer.

It is worth pointing out that the $5,000 cost of delivery (which translates into $0.025 per email) is a campaign-oriented way of accounting for the cost. In a program scenario, we don't count cost per contact. Instead, we look at a blended cost of all customer communication. This is a more complicated calculation, but one that normally results in an even lower cost per contact if it were broken out separately.

BUILDING LASTING LOYALTY

Creating loyalty is the most powerful way to retain customers. Although it's possible to retain customers who are not loyal, the relationship you have with them is fragile and they're likely to take their business elsewhere in a heartbeat. We've already discussed many of the nonproduct factors that affect loyalty: building service relationships, knowing your customers so you can anticipate their needs, establishing a foundation of trust. Here are several other email marketing programs and techniques that are used either separately or in combination to acquire, convert, or retain loyal customers.

COMMUNITY

Creating a sense of belonging and encouraging active participation in a group of individuals with similar interests is a powerful way to create loyalty and retain customers. Email communities are usually services or programs—most often discussion groups—that enable individuals to communicate with each other through email. Everyone who signs up for a particular discussion group or topic receives all the email that is sent to the group. Some topics may contain sponsorship (commercial) messages; others may not. Companies such as eGroups (acquired by Yahoo!) and LifeMinders specialize in creating email communities.

You can use email communities to create a place where your customers can discuss your products or services. These forums can be powerful retention tools because they create community and build loyalty, not only to your company but to your customer base as well. Company-sponsored forums can also build trust by showing your customers that you have nothing to hide. But be careful: Forums are difficult to moderate or control, so don't create or facilitate one unless you're comfortable exposing your customers to bad feelings and experiences along with the good ones.

REWARDS PROGRAMS

If you're a member of even one frequent-flyer program, you know that once you begin to accumulate points and take advantage of the upgrades, free trips, and other benefits, choosing a carrier becomes an irrational process. In the name of earning miles, many people fly on their mileage program airline even if the flights are more expensive or less convenient.

You can encourage certain behaviors by integrating rewards into email programs. You might, for example, give away points such as ClickMiles (from the ClickRewards loyalty program [www.ClickRewards.com]), to encourage recipients to tell their friends and colleagues about special offers or programs they should sign up for. Every time they forward the email to somebody and that person signs up for a program or makes a purchase, the one who forwarded the message earns points. You might want to consider developing a rewards program in conjunction with your email program. Imagine that people automatically get 500 points just for signing up. After that, they continue to earn points as long as they stay engaged: For instance they would receive 10 points every time they open one of your emails, 20 more for responding (clicking on a link), and 1 point for every dollar they spend.

Email is also useful for making customers aware of their reward status and encouraging them to return to your site to redeem their awards or to earn extra points on a limited-time offer or simply to buy more to reach a new level. An individual customer's reward status is an effective element you can use to personalize communication. Knowing what level your customers are at lets you tailor the voice, content, and offer to each customer.

KickStart.com (www.kickstart.com) is one example of how a company can combine both community and rewards to retain members. KickStart is a "portal with a cause," providing a home page tailored to various organizations such as Mile High United Way, Cheerleaders Association of America, Promise Keepers, and many others. These organizations, in turn, encourage their members to sign up for KickStart. The cheerleaders at a local high school, for instance, find out about the service from their national association. The local chapter creates a KickStart home page, and the cheerleaders tell their friends and family to support them by making KickStart their default home page, which they can personalize as they like. If you decide to support your daughter's cheerleading squad by switching to KickStart, you can access email, view stock quotes, get news updates, and take advantage of a number of other services that Internet users have come to expect from personal home pages such as MyYahoo! and MyExcite. But unlike other personal home pages, the KickStart page will contain a section devoted to the local chapter you supported by signing up with KickStart in the first place. Organizations can, of course, update the information their supporters see as often as they like. For infrequent Web users or those who opt not to make KickStart their home page, KickStart operates an email newsletter service that delivers news, offers, and information directly by email.

The community factor means that whether you visit your own home page or receive the newsletter, you'll know it contains not only your personal preferences, but information about your daughter's cheerleading chapter. KickStart also creates incentives with its powerful reward structure: A substantial portion of all advertising, affiliate program, and sponsorship revenue generated from the use of the service is paid out to the organizations that users are associated with. KickStart rewards loyal use by giving money to the organization or charity of the users' choice.

EMAIL NEWSLETTERS

These are perhaps the most common vehicles for establishing ongoing dialogue with customers, probably because they provide a terrific mechanism for communicating a highly personalized blend of information, entertainment, and promotions.

One online natural health products company has developed a very effective newsletter. As soon as customers sign up they begin to receive information about the categories they selected. And as they begin to make purchases, the company adjusts the components of the newsletter to suggest products that are natural complements to what the customers have already purchased. The company made a conscious decision to cap the promotional content of the newsletter at 30 percent. By keeping the bulk of the content relevant and original (it's written by an independent editorial staff as well as outside health professionals) the company has made its newsletter a valued source of information. And by carefully targeting promotional offers to the context of past purchases, the company ensures very high response and conversion rates, which enables them to cost-justify the overall program.

How you position your newsletter is an important exercise in consumer research and branding—and it can have a big impact on the overall success of your email marketing program. In some cases you'll want to produce an ordinary or traditional newsletter. Other times you might be better off with a tips-and-tricks or high-level weekly summary approach with links pointing back to more information. Positioning your communications in ways that make it easy for subscribers to understand the value they will receive is important. I recently met with a company that had developed a very interesting travel-related Internet service. They wanted to develop an email newsletter to keep in touch with their members. After some discussion it became clear that the last thing travelers are looking for is "yet another travel newsletter." The challenge was to develop and brand an exciting communications service that delivered unique value. They realized that by sending fewer communications, while staying focused on the core value they delivered, they'd have a much more valuable email program if they just sent out a generic (nonpersonalized) travel newsletter every week.

EMAIL ALERTS

Sending an email alert whenever something occurs that is of interest to a customer creates a relationship built on reliance and anticipation. An email alert can have real value. For example, a customer may receive an alert that a stock he owns just hit a record high, that a product he owns is being recalled, that week-end tickets to Mexico are on sale for the next three hours, or that an online auction is about to close. Relevant, timely alerts demonstrate that when your company speaks, it's worth listening. They also show that you have the customer's best interests at heart.

UP-SELL AND CROSS-SELL

Consider the difference between the following messages,

- "Thank you for your recent purchase. Here is a $10 coupon redeemable at our store in the next 30 days." This is a standard, incentive-based promotional email. It may generate decent response rates (10 percent or more), but the promotion will be expensive to run, especially if you are selling low-cost, low-margin items.
- "We've noticed that you recently bought two books on how to restore antique cars and thought you might be interested in owning a copy of *The Complete Encyclopedia of Antique Automobiles.*" This is an up-sell. It doesn't offer a discount because the context of the offer is so relevant.
- "We've noticed that you recently bought two books on how to restore antique cars and thought you might be interested in *A History of Antique Watches.*" This is a cross-sell. It gives the recipient an opportunity to buy a product or service in a different but related category.

Up-sell and cross-sell messages can be delivered as separate emails or they can be incorporated into other communications, such as newsletters. Either way, done right they are an excellent tool that can increase the chances that customers who make a first purchase will make others.

The examples above illustrate how to develop a cross-sell and up-sell in the context of past purchases. Most recipients will find this type of communication fun, amusing, interesting, and helpful, whether they respond or not. But there can be a downside, particularly if your messages are purely promotional. You may think a 10 percent response rate on an up-sell promotion is great, but it's sometimes worthwhile to keep in mind that you're also getting a 90 percent *nonresponse* rate. And chances are that a large percentage of those nonresponders are finding your messages annoying.

REMINDER AND GIFT SUGGESTION SERVICES

Petopia (www.petopia.com) runs a birthday reminder and gift suggestion program for its customers' pets, which takes into consideration the type of pet the customer owns, the time of year, and other factors. This type of program can naturally be expanded to cover a wide variety of applications, such as birthday reminders for family, friends, and colleagues, anniversaries, special holiday reminders, wedding gift suggestions, and more. Reminders and suggestion services are great because they encourage customers to tell you something about themselves that you can then use to provide them with better service and value.

WIN-BACK PROGRAMS

Given that it's more expensive to acquire new customers than to retain existing ones, e-retailers and service providers should do whatever they can to avoid losing customers or win them back if they leave. The natural starting point for developing a win-back program is to understand what's causing customers to disengage in the first place. Data analysis may reveal common characteristics of likely defectors, but it won't tell you how to reengage them. You can use email to reach out and invite these customers to participate in a study designed to reveal the reasons they are disengaging. Once you understand their reasons, the next step is to design an email-based outreach program that promises to address their concerns or grievances. The very act of engaging with customers, asking for their feedback, and then demonstrating that you're willing to make changes has often been very successful in converting even the most disgruntled customers into loyal believers.

OTHER EMAIL MARKETING PROGRAMS

Here are a few other email marketing programs and services that don't fit quite so neatly under the acquisition, conversion, retention labels.

SALES COMMUNICATION

Whenever a customer makes a purchase online she should immediately receive a confirmation email. Once the product ships, she should receive another email telling her so and possibly including UPS, Fed Ex, or other tracking numbers. Integrate these purchase-related emails with your email marketing program because a purchase confirmation is a prime opportunity to up-sell or cross-sell. These notices may also be good places to start building or reinforcing a brand relationship by inviting new customers to engage in a broader email marketing program or thanking repeat customers for their continued loyalty.

CUSTOMER SERVICE AND SUPPORT

There is no better place to make customers loyal for life—or lose them forever—than during their interactions with your customer support operation. If a customer sends you an email with a complaint or a request for help, you have an opportunity to engage him in a highly individualized dialogue. Once his issues have been positively resolved, a follow-up email can help ensure that he's satisfied. The follow-up might even offer a token of appreciation for having been so patient—another powerful way to ensure that he feels properly looked after and well cared for. In addition, when customers call your 1-800-support number, you have a perfect opportunity to ask for their email addresses and permission to contact them later online.

POINT-OF-SALE SUPPORT

Consider a traditional retail experience: You hear that Neiman Marcus is having a sale because you receive a handwritten note from the salesperson you bought something from six months ago. You show up at the store and within minutes, a friendly, helpful salesperson asks you whether she can help you. If it's the same one who served you last time, she may even recognize you and greet you by name. Maybe you feel like browsing or maybe you need some help finding what you want. The in-store retail experience has been designed to accommodate either of these modes.

But does your website do the same? Can your customers respond to your email with a question and get a quick response? Can they engage with someone at your website through an instant messaging program or have someone call them with the information they need? A little human contact can make a big difference. Victoria's Secret discovered that of the people who buy something within ten days of receiving an email marketing message, a high percentage make the actual purchase over the phone. The company's assumption is that many of these people buy offline because of the increased service level that a human being can offer.

Finally, make it easy for your customers to buy! This may sound painfully obvious, but it is astounding how many online retailers do just the opposite. Does clicking on a link in an email you send out take the customer directly to the product or service you're promoting? Even better, does it link the product directly to the customer's shopping cart or does it leave him lost on your home page? Personally if I got an email from you I would be extremely disappointed if I clicked through to your site and had to spend time and effort to find the product I was interested in, put it in the shopping cart, and so on. When a customer receives an email, the call to action must be obvious and clear, and following it should never take more than one or two clicks.

INTEGRATING ONLINE AND OFFLINE PROGRAMS

No marketing program is an island. There will often be overlap between marketing and advertising campaigns run offline and online. Below we take a look at several different ways that offline and online direct marketing programs can be designed to leverage each other.

EMAIL PROMOTION WITH OFFLINE FULFILLMENT

A financial services company might send prospects an email offer to open an online brokerage account. Within the email there could be a question asking the recipient whether he or she would like to submit an application online through the Web, have a fax automatically deliver with the necessary forms and information, receive a sign-up package in the mail, or have an actual customer service person fill in the application over the phone. Depending on the answer, a browser would open up asking for the appropriate information needed to process the request.

POSTCARD MAILER WITH UNIQUE ID AND ONLINE FOLLOW-UP

A company that runs an online game service might send a postcard offering a free month of service to households that a third-party company such as Naviant (www.naviant.com) has indicated are likely to be online. (Naviant has a database of over 175 million Internet-enabled households, and companies using its services can select a detailed customer segment based on any number of demographic attributes.) When card recipients arrive at the special Web address, they're prompted to type in their email addresses and the special codes printed on the cards and to indicate whether they'd like to receive emails when new online games are released. The code printed on each card is unique to each recipient and is used to connect the email address with a user. Follow-up emails can use the known information from the offline database to personalize and target the content of the emails, increasing the relevance of the messages and the likelihood of response.

DEAD EMAIL POSTCARDS

Over the course of a year, 15 to 25 percent of your company's database of customer email addresses will become stale or unreachable. This is a function of a number of factors, such as customers changing their email address or unsubscribing from your program. One way to avoid this problem is to encourage your customers to keep their personal profiles up to date. Another way is to send snail-mail postcards to reach out to customers with dead email addresses, letting them know you've been trying to contact them, and ask for an update. The postage-paid card should contain the old email address and leave an opening for the recipient to fill in a new one. As soon as you receive a return response, update your database with the new address and send an automatic "welcome back and thank you" message. By email, of course.

ONLINE TESTING FOR OFFLINE CAMPAIGNS

In traditional direct mail, getting response data from a marketing campaign can easily take six weeks. Online, though, 90 percent of the responses to any given email marketing campaign usually come within the first several days. That makes using email a great way to test your offline direct marketing campaign, allowing you to try several versions of a program, compare results, and make adjustments— all within days (e.g., $20.00 off vs. 20% off vs. "free shipping").

Online testing works especially well for organizations with large databases of customers and prospects but email addresses for only a small portion of them. Assuming that you have enough email addresses for a statistically significant sample, once the email test results make it clear which offers will work best with which groups, the lists for the full-scale mail campaign can be extracted using the same demographic selectors as the email. When doing this kind of testing be sure to pay close attention to the permission and opt-in rules outlined in this book.

DIRECT-RESPONSE MAIL WITH AUTOMATIC EMAIL FOLLOW-UP

In theory, companies can gather a lot of customer information from product registrations. More often than not, though, none of this information makes its way out of the product registration database. One reason for this is that it's expensive to send follow-up mail to every customer who registers. But if you're doing business online, it should be a crime not to design new-product registration cards with a field that asks for email address. Once customers opt-in on their product registration cards to receive information, you have a phenomenal opportunity to use the cost advantages of email to stay in touch with them on a regular basis.

INTEGRATED CONTACT MIX

In some cases you may want to integrate mail, phone, and email contacts in one approach. A magazine publisher, for example, might use email to make the initial contact with people whose subscriptions are about to expire. If there is no response within a week, the company might send out a renewal offer by regular mail. That could be followed by a second mail offer, which in turn could be followed by a phone call. If there's still no response, the company might send yet another email and repeat the process either until the subscriber renews or indicates (possibly by ignoring all these attempts to get in touch) that he or she doesn't intend to renew.

You can test different sequences to help you develop the optimal contact approach for each subscriber segment. Once the customer has renewed, though, email is the perfect medium to use to say thanks and to offer additional services, such as daily, weekly, monthly, or subscribers-only email updates. And when developing marketing programs that span mail and phone, be sure to integrate all your databases. A customer who responds to a campaign online should not later get the same offer by mail.

DEVELOPING INTEGRATED CROSS-CHANNEL PROGRAMS

Your customers don't see you as having "channels." To them you're a single brand. And whether shopping in your retail store, calling you on the telephone, or engaging with you on the Internet, they expect you to recognize them in the same way: as *the customer*. OfficeMax (www.officemax.com) understands this quite well and is building a comprehensive customer marketing program that spans all its channels: storefronts, direct mail, and e-commerce. The goal is to develop a customer database that enables the company to determine the best way to serve each customer. Some want to receive all Office-Max communication by email but will make their purchases in retail stores. Others may want to conduct all their business online. Office-Max wants to leave it up to the customer to set the parameters for how they communicate and do business with the company. They are tracking how different customers respond to various forms of communication and tailoring their approaches to individual customer response patterns.

Wegmans Food Markets (www.wegmans.com) is listed by *Fortune* magazine among the 60 largest private companies in the United States. Unlike such Web-based food merchants as Web Van and Peapod, Wegmans provides no home delivery service. Personal service is a central element of the Wegmans experience and the company wants people to come into the stores and shop. Wegmans online presence and email marketing program are designed to complement the customer's in-store experience.

The goal of the program is to help customers plan their family's meals for the week. Wegmans wants to know its customers and everyone else in the family. It wants to know each customer's dietary constraints and the foods they prefer. Using this knowledge, Wegmans will deliver an email every Monday morning with a personalized family meal plan for the week. The meal plan suggests prepared meals that match the family's specific requirements. Naturally, the email alerts shoppers to specials at their local store. It may also make suggestions and include recipes for nonprepared meals and provide an itemized shopping list (complete with aisle numbers) that busy shoppers can print out and bring with them when they swing by the store on their way home from work.

To track the success and maximize the effectiveness of cross-channel programs, it is important to record and integrate all customer interactions, regardless of the channel they occur in. Nearly 80 percent of Wegmans customers, for example, pay for their purchases with a Wegmans card. This means that the company can track the email marketing program's success and continuously improve the service it provides by correlating its emails to each customer's specific purchase patterns.

This chapter has given you a thorough overview of what you and your company can do with email and how you might use it to build relationships through the establishment of an ongoing dialogue with your customers. But that's not the end of the story. Far from it. In the next chapters of this book, we will be spending a lot of time exploring how to design and implement an email marketing program.

CHAPTER 4

STRATEGIC PLANNING LEADS TO RAPID IMPLEMENTATION

S O YOU'VE DECIDED you should email your customers and you're ready to put together your marketing program. Great. But before you start worrying about implementation you'll need to spend some time planning things out. Everything happens so fast on the Internet and too many companies rush through the process of planning their Internet direct marketing programs. Don't make this mistake. When it comes to email marketing programs, planning and implementation are equally important, and cutting corners on either will hurt the whole program. A well-thought-out plan can be implemented rapidly, but implementing your plan before you've spent enough time working out the details will ultimately slow you down.

There are two basic approaches to email marketing: tactical and strategic. The *tactical approach* involves little more than "just sending" your customers some email. These programs are short-term focused and not integrated into the overall marketing strategy. Maybe you're doing it because your competition is doing it. Maybe you think email is a cost-effective mechanism for broadcasting offers to your customers. Or maybe you aren't meeting your quarterly targets and you hope that a blanket email campaign will bring in extra revenue.

The problem with the tactical approach is that it doesn't place email in the context of your broader business goals. It doesn't consider email's true value or the potentially negative consequences of sending emails to your customers. At the very least, a tactical approach will keep you from maximizing your customers' full revenue potential. More likely, though, you'll alienate some of your best customers and destroy relationships with others, get cited for privacy violations, and cause irreparable harm to your public brand image.

The *strategic approach*, on the other hand, considers and carefully plans out such goals as increasing customer loyalty, creating lasting customer relationships, improving repeat purchase rates and satisfaction, and increasing revenues and profitability. A comprehensive strategy considers the consequences of the email program and ensures that your goals can be achieved without compromising any important element of your business.

MAPPING YOUR EMAIL MARKETING PROGRAMS TO DEFINED BUSINESS GOALS AND OBJECTIVES

The first step in your strategic-planning process is to consider the kinds of questions listed below. Your answers to these questions are a reflection of the strategic goals and objectives you've defined for your business. If you don't understand or can't articulate these goals, you won't be able to identify the criteria that will determine whether your program is a success or a failure.

- Why are you interested in email marketing in the first place? (Are you trying to bring in new revenue? Reduce costs? Are competitive pressures forcing you to consider email?)
- Is long-term customer retention important for the success of your business?
- Is it important and possible to measure your program's impact on customer loyalty?
- If you can expect to make a sale to your customers only once a year, can you justify the expense of the program?
- Why would your customers be interested in receiving your emails?
- What kinds of material are they going to want? (Strictly educational? Business related? New product or upgrade informa-

tion? Will you inform them if a competitive offering becomes available?)

- Will your customers look to you as an authoritative, trusted source of information, or will they always consider what you do and say as simply serving your own needs in an attempt to sell them more products or services?
- How much information will they give you about themselves?
- How much can you learn by observing their activities on the website, responding to their email, and analyzing their purchasing activity?

DEVELOPING A CUSTOMER CONTACT PLAN

A contact plan describes in specific detail how you will contact prospects and customers over a period of time to meet your specific goals. Each contact plan should contain the following sections:

A WRITTEN CONTACT STRATEGY

Your contact strategy spells out your goals and describes how ongoing customer communication will be used to meet those goals. When thinking about your contact strategy, be sure to consider the online service imperative that we discussed in Chapter 1. What are you going to offer your existing and prospective customers in exchange for giving you permission to contact them? When Wegmans Food Markets developed its contact strategy, it focused on extending the service and customer-oriented approach that you'll find in its retail stores to email communication. It has developed a contact strategy that is focused more on delivering relevant content and information than on selling. Its goal is to ensure that it provides its customers with notification of special produce, recipes, health tips, and more in order to simplify their grocery shopping and food preparation tasks.

Wells Fargo Bank's small business group uses email in a comparable manner. Its goal is to provide a helpful service to its small business customers by informing and educating. Its contact strategy includes book reviews, tax information, and offers for additional value-added services. A somewhat different approach is taken by EGreetings.com (www.egreetings.com), the Internet greeting cards service. Its contact strategy is to focus on tapping into its large user base to deliver product and service promotions on behalf of other advertisers. It sends targeted promotions in addition to delivering content and information regarding its own site.

And then there is wildbrain.com (www.wildbrain.com), the online division of WildBrain, Inc., one of the country's largest animation studios. wildbrain.com's strategy at this point is to develop an audience for its Web-based animation episodes, which it calls "webisodes." It sends amusing and entertaining animated email alerts that invite people who have signed up to view the latest webisode.

Because a lot of people will probably be collaborating on your contact strategy, it should be in writing and very detailed. That way you can be sure that your strategic framework and the goals of the program are shared by everyone.

PROGRAM OFFERINGS

What programs does your site offer to men in their late thirties, women in their early twenties, busy professional mothers, or empty nesters? Understanding which of your products and services appeals to specific market segments is critical to the success of your email marketing programs. It will drive all your efforts to personalize both the email and website experience for visitors, prospects, and returning customers.

By developing distinct program offerings you'll be making it easier for your subscribers to get value from your email marketing programs. You'll undoubtedly want to offer sale notifications to your customers during your company's biannual sale, for example. To do so you may develop a separate program offering called Sale Notifications and allow customers to opt-in or out. You can further refine this offering by deciding that certain segments don't need to be told about sales at all. You might, for example, send people you know are simply not price-sensitive timely, useful replenishment notifications and updates when certain new products and styles are introduced.

Let's take a look at a hypothetical company, Lola's Lingerie. The following chart shows a matrix of five lifestyle-oriented customer segments and five possible program offerings.

PROGRAM OFFERINGS

	Type of Customer	Romantic Tips	Gift Services	Sale Notifications	Style Guides	Recommendations
CUSTOMER SEGMENTS	Romantic	X	X			X
	Busy professional		X	X	X	X
	Nonbuyer (brand)	X			X	
	Seeking inspiration	X			X	X
	Bargain hunter			X		X

There is, of course, some overlap, but this kind of chart clearly demonstrates the need for tailoring specific program offerings to specific segments.

As you might guess, gender plays an important role here and is critical in helping define the type of communication you'll have with your customers. The Romantic segment, for example, is geared mostly toward men. The services offered are therefore focused on romantic tips, gift services, and recommendations. A service that provided style guides would be less interesting to the male segment but might appeal to the busy professional woman.

A MESSAGE PLAN

Once you have segmented your customers and defined separate program offerings, you'll be able to create and manage the different contacts that each segment should receive as well as determine how frequently to send messages. You'll want to create individualized message plans that allow you to deliver a personalized, timed, and sequenced stream of communication to each customer.

Based on the segmentations above, Lola's Lingerie would want to implement a message plan around gift reminders and suggestions. This plan, which would be primarily geared to the male segment, would identify relevant events and dates such as Valentine's Day, Mother's Day, wife or girlfriend's birthday, etc. and specify an appropriate sequence of messages designed to service the male segment. Petopia might develop a message plan specifically geared toward dog owners who live in large cities. It would tell them about dog walks in the city, helping introduce and bring together communities of like-minded pet owners.

CONTACT DRIVERS

What kinds of things will trigger contact? In some instances you'll plan and schedule your contacts far in advance (such as annual sales). Others times you'll be responding to one of the following situations:

- *Consumer requests contact.* A customer might sign up to receive a personalized monthly newsletter or send an email asking about a new product you're selling. When a new subscriber signs up for eHarlequin.com's newsletter program, she immediately receives a welcome message confirming what she's signed up for and ensuring that she will know how to modify her personal preferences if she should ever decide to change the content she wants to receive. When eBags receives an email inquiry from a customer, a skilled customer service professional looks up any relevant information and answers all My eBags membership, product, or order-related questions by email within 12 to 24 hours. An inbound email from a customer regarding an order the customer would like to return even triggers a series of follow-up emails that are automatically delivered within a few days of each other. These follow-up emails ensure that the customer's product return is picked up, and that a replacement order is processed satisfactorily.
- *Customer action initiates contact.* A customer makes a purchase and you automatically send out an order confirmation that contains a personalized coupon for 10 percent off the next purchase. For instance, if you buy something at Barnes and

Noble's website and you're a member of the ClickRewards program, you may receive a follow-on email notifying you that you will be awarded extra bonus points if you are deemed to be a loyal customer (which is based on such factors as how often you buy, when you made your last purchase, and how much money you've spent over the total relationship you've had with the company). Or imagine that a customer clicks on a link in an email and gets taken to a mortgage loan application. If she exits the site without filling out the form, the company might send her an email a week later containing an application that takes less time to submit (working off the assumption that the customer didn't fill out the form because it was too long).

- *Customer-related events initiate contact.* You might send your customers special notes on their birthdays thanking them for their business. Or a customer's change of address might trigger a contact sequence from a retailer in the home furnishings business. SpringStreet is a website for apartment rentals. It knows when people move and where they move to and it uses this information to deliver highly relevant and timely emails with special offers and useful information, such as a checklist of organizations to contact with their new address.

- *External events initiate contact.* Three feet of fresh powder on a nearby mountain may trigger sporting goods retailers to let customers who've bought ski equipment know that it might be time for a new pair of skis. Other events—from product recalls and updates to major fashion shows—can also spark this kind of timely notification. CDNOW gets a great response from sending its customers emails alerting them that their favorite artists are coming to town. Its customers see it as a value-added benefit, proof that CDNOW actually cares about them, not just an attempt to sell them something.

A MESSAGE TEST PLAN

The last step in the process of creating your contact plan is to come up with a plan for testing the quality and performance of individual messages as well as ongoing campaigns. The test plan outlines the criteria that must be met and describes the methods for collecting the data and feedback that will be used to determine the program's success or failure. For instance, before Illuminations (www.illuminations.com), a retailer with physical stores, a catalogue and a website that all sell a large variety of high-quality candles, launched its email program, it wanted to compare the effectiveness of HTML email to plain-text email. It confirmed that HTML email performed more than twice as well (as measured both in terms of response rate and sales) as plain-text email and decided to make an up-front investment in developing HTML email capabilities as a part of its email program.

You can break your message testing plan into two separate categories: ongoing tests and one-time tests.

Ongoing tests assess the quality, reliability, and performance of new and ongoing programs. Email messages are first sent out to a "seed list," a representative sample of virtual customers. This will enable you to review the layout, formatting, URLs (links), personalization, and so on, of the emails that are being delivered. The seed list should contain email addresses hosted by a range of ISPs, making it possible to test different programs such as free Web-based email services, plain text email programs, AOL email, Eudora, and Microsoft Exchange. The customer data for the seed list should also contain a mix of data that exercises all variants of personalization. For instance, if the email is personalized based on gender, it is important that both men and women (as well as customers who did not specify their gender) receive the message. Before an email is delivered to the actual customer base, the seed list is targeted and a group of designated testers picks up the emails that have been mailed out and carefully inspects them to make sure they were delivered correctly and contain no errors.

Ongoing tests are also used to monitor the performance of a given program. They offer a baseline against which to measure the success of your program over time. One way to perform an ongoing test is to define a control group that gets excluded from select email programs or campaigns. By comparing their activity with those who participate in the email program you'll be able to measure precisely how effective your program is. Another ongoing test is to define a control group that receives a subset of your emails, for instance, only the promotional emails but not the informational emails. This allows you to measure the long-term impact of a blended contact mix on customer retention and customer value.

One-time tests are designed to test limited-duration or one-time marketing programs. One-time tests are also very helpful when designing and planning new campaigns. The mechanics of implementing and executing a one-time test are similar to those of the ongoing test plan. For example, Amazon.com may run a one-time test to see if people who have purchased auto repair books are likely to be interested in coffee table books on antique cars. Or, an Internet apartment rental service might develop a one-time test to see how different customer segments respond to an email newsletter designed to provide information and relevant promotions for people who have just moved to a new apartment. A one-time test might be used to determine whether the newsletter will generate a better response if its content is personalized based on the recipient's city as well as other information gathered from the recipient's demographic profile (data submitted at the time of the initial apartment search). Different designs and different levels of personalization can be tested to measure their impact. It may be possible to quantify the value that a highly personalized newsletter will generate, thereby justifying the additional cost of running the program. (We will discuss how to actually measure and track the success of a program in greater detail in Chapter 8.)

THE STRATEGIC INVESTMENT PERSPECTIVE

It takes a long-term financial commitment to run an ongoing customer communications program. Although the incremental cost of contacting customers online is close to zero, the fixed costs of developing and operating an email relationship marketing program can be significant. If your company's goals are driven exclusively by short-term revenue opportunities, promotional, campaign-oriented emails will probably be the most cost-effective way to go. Or if you do not know how well your customers will respond to receiving your email, you may want to begin with some basic campaigns. For instance, when Illuminations decided to first dip its toes into the email marketing waters, it did so by doing a single-test campaign. It performed above expectations and proved to the company that email was going to be a powerful tool for its future marketing, so it decided to make a long-term investment in direct customer communication through email.

If your company's primary goal is to realize long-term gains from your customers and engage them in a lasting dialogue, you're going to incur significant planning, development and maintenance costs. Illuminations quickly figured out that it needed an integrated email marketing program, so it implemented a full email relationship marketing program, delivering regularly scheduled, personalized communication. Illuminations' strategic investment is paying off handsomely. In the fourth quarter of 1999, its email program exceeded its ambitious revenue goals.

The fixed costs associated with maintaining a strategic customer communication and marketing program can be justified a number of different ways. (For a more detailed discussion of different ways that organizations can develop financial models for justifying their expenditures in customer-centered marketing programs, see ROI discussion later in this chapter.)

TOP-LINE VS. BOTTOM-LINE IMPACT

Email marketing programs can affect a company's finances in two different ways. A program's *top-line impact* measures its contribution to gross revenue. In other words, it evaluates the program's effectiveness by determining whether customers are buying more frequently and spending more on each purchase as a direct result of having received an email communication. Of course, to figure out exactly what the top-line impact is, you'll need to be able to track the revenue that can be directly attributed to your email marketing program. When Victoria's Secret sends email to customers or prospects, it tracks every purchase those people make—either on the Web or by telephone—for ten days after they receive the email. This enables the company to measure the impact of its email communication, even if customers don't make a purchase the exact moment an email arrives.

Bottom-line impact, on the other hand, measures the savings a particular program generates, especially relative to other types of programs. Imagine, for example, that your organization wants to send out a quarterly newsletter to your 750,000 customers. The cost of sending out a hard-copy newsletter might be as follows:

Newsletter copy and content development	$7,000
Newsletter design and production	2,000
Printing costs (@ $0.40 per copy)	300,000
Postage (@ $0.20 per copy)	150,000
Total	$459,000

The cost of sending out an email-only newsletter would be closer to this:

Newsletter copy and content development (w/personalization)	$10,000
Newsletter design and production (w/personalization)	4,000
Email delivery and tracking (monthly cost)	30,000
Total	$44,000

In the above example, an email newsletter costs less than 10 percent of a printed one. But the economics of email get even better the more you communicate. If you wanted to a second edition of the printed newsletter, you'd incur most of the $459,000 costs again. But with the email newsletter, the $30,000 monthly charge (which is what a service provider might charge for a typical ongoing program) is essentially the cost for operating the *entire* email marketing program. Once the program is in place, you can contact your customers as often as is appropriate without any increase in your monthly expenses. Instead of producing a single issue of a newsletter for about half a million dollars every quarter, you could develop a continuous customer communications program for about one-fourth the cost. There are, of course, some one-time set-up and design costs that aren't included in the above figures. But if these costs are amortized over the duration of the marketing program, they become practically negligible. Before Palm Inc. first began operating its

InSync Online email program, it sent a regular quarterly newsletter to all its registered customers at a cost of approximately $250,000 per mailing (that's over $1 million a year). After only a few months of operating the Insync program, Palm discontinued the printed newsletter because Insync was able to deliver much more relevant, timely, and personalized content at just a fraction of the newsletter cost per year.

INVESTING IN PEOPLE AND KNOWLEDGE

To run a successful email marketing program (or any other strategic marketing or business program, for that matter), you need to make an active investment in people. But because email marketing is a relatively new practice, it's going to be difficult to hire people with actual experience in the field. There are several service organizations that can provide solutions for organizations willing to outsource their email marketing programs (we discuss some of them in Chapter 10). But even if you outsource your program, your internal marketing people will still have to direct and manage the service provider, which means that you'll probably have to develop some of your own expertise and knowledge in-house. Homestore.com for example, has a dedicated email marketing manager who manages the company's relationship with its email marketing service provider. This person is responsible for coordinating all internal technical and marketing resources with the service provider. He's also responsible for managing all email communication with Homestore.com's customers across it's six real estate–related sister sites, including SpringStreet.com, REALTOR.com®, and HomeFair.com.

Because every business is different and has unique needs, organizational structures, and requirements, there is no simple lineup of people you'll need for your email relationship marketing program. Suffice it to say, though, they will have to be skilled, creative, and dedicated. There's also no simple solution for finding these people, but in Chapter 7 we take a more detailed look at staffing and resource planning, and we discuss the various positions you will need to fill to run a successful program.

DEVELOPING A RETURN-ON-INVESTMENT MODEL

How much are your customers worth to you? How much long-term revenue do you lose when a customer comes to your website and doesn't buy anything or perhaps buys something but never comes back? Sadly, far too many companies can't answer these questions. Why? Because it requires that they capture, track, and analyse mountains of customer data over time. Understanding what data to capture and coordinating the integration of appropriate customer data from multiple sources is difficult and expensive. Even when it's possible to access and collect the required information, it's often a challenge to get executives to dedicate the resources necessary to measure the long-term value of customers and the cost associated with *not* maximizing that value.

The figure on the next page illustrates a basic model for measuring the return on investment of an email marketing program. It shows the type of information an organization needs in order to measure its ROI. It tracks two types of customer value: (1) *purchase value* which is the average purchase price times the expected number of purchases over the lifetime of the customer relationship; and (2) *community and referral value,* which is the advertising revenue generated by exposing the customer to promotions plus the referral value generated from clicking through on links to third-party marketing and commerce partners. The combination of the purchase value and the community and referral value is the "click value," which is discussed in Chapter 8 as part of a more detailed discussion about measuring and tracking customer value online.

Measuring the ROI of your email marketing program requires that you know how much it costs you to acquire each new customer, the cost of operating a retention marketing program, and the expected long-term value of a customer. Knowing the expected value of your customers or website visitors allows you to make better decisions about how much to spend on acquisition and retention. By developing an ROI model for your email marketing program you'll begin to understand and justify where to allocate your marketing dollars.

The model in the illustration gives an overall picture of the ROI

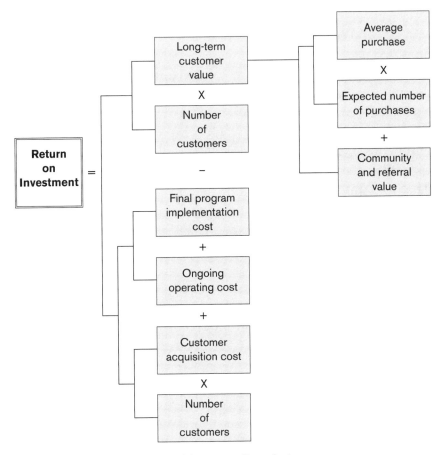

Basic ROI model for an email marketing program.

for an entire program, but it doesn't describe how individual customer segments might impact a particular program. Some segments cost more to service than others because of the level of support they demand. Others segments may be highly profitable and price-insensitive. Understanding how individual customer segments impact the ROI will be especially important as we develop a more sophisticated and sensitive model that enables marketers to control important parameters such as revenue and profitability while operating their email marketing program.

When N2K (the online music retailer that merged with CDNOW in 1999) analyzed its MyMusicBoulevard customer data it realized that over half of its sales were in the rock-and-roll genre. These were also the least profitable customers that N2K had, mainly buying sale CDs from the Top 100 charts. To make things worse, rock-and-roll customers were always looking for the best price and were not very loyal to MusicBoulevard. The ROI on this customer segment was very poor. Approximately 30 percent of the MusicBoulevard customers had a very different profile. They were older and not very price-sensitive, looking instead for selection and convenience; they made most of their purchases in jazz, blues, and classical music, typically much higher margin genres. Once these people made their first purchase, they were very likely to buy again if they received carefully considered emails with offers and information about the kind of music they'd expressed interest in.

DESIGNING A ROAD MAP

How are you going to evolve your customer contact strategy over time? Which priorities are immediate and which are long-term? What resources can you expect to get right away and what are the hurdles you have to cross before you can broaden your initiative? These questions and others like them are best answered by designing a road map that will help you set and meet your expectations.

By developing a road map that highlights dependencies among functions in your program and your investment and resource needs, you will be able to understand, prioritize, and plan for anything that might impact either performance or functionality. For instance, if you find that it will be difficult and expensive to integrate purchase information into customer profiles, this will affect your ability to segment, personalize, and, perhaps most important, measure the financial impact and ROI of your programs.

Take, for example, the natural health products webstore that started its email program with two newsletters. One was mostly informational and the other was promotional. But while customers and prospects could sign up to receive one or both, everyone would receive the same content and promotional offers. It was important to the health products company that it get up and running and start communicating with customers quickly but without placing an initial burden on its internal IT resources. For that reason, the company's road map indicated that limited data was going to be made available for the initial program launch. Within several months of launching the initial program, though, the company had begun incorporating detailed purchase information into the email marketing data mart. (We talk more about data marts in Chapter 5.) This information enabled the company to target and personalize its emails based on each customer's purchases (number and actual products). Equally important, the natural health products site could now easily measure and track the effectiveness of its programs by running detailed reports that incorporated response and purchase activity. Had this company tried to implement the entire program in one go, it might very well have run into unpredictable hurdles. Instead, it developed a road map prioritizing the marketing goals of the program and an implementation plan to support those goals.

Your road map is your tool for understanding and explaining what your program is capable of doing over time, and it will be invaluable when you're establishing priorities. It's easy to lose track of what has to happen immediately and what falls into the "nice to have" category. A well-designed road map lets you schedule and prioritize all the elements of your program, including the resources you need to ensure its successful implementation and operation.

It may just sound like plain old common sense to make plans before setting out on a journey, but you'd be surprised how many companies start trying to communicate with their customers on the Internet before they've clearly articulated their goals. Unless you have a firm understanding of what you want to do, you'll never be able to determine which data to collect and store. By carefully and strategically setting goals and planning your email direct marketing programs you can avoid time-consuming delays and keep your customers happy. In the next chapter we discuss not only how to evaluate your data needs but how to gather the richest data in the most effective ways.

CHAPTER 5

THE POWER OF
CUSTOMER DATA

I N NO OTHER MEDIUM has there ever been as much data available about users, prospects, or customers as there is on the Internet, and all of it is available to marketers in real time. That can be a good thing or a bad thing. High-traffic websites can easily generate giga-bytes of data every day, but no one can possibly use all of it, and, frankly, most people wouldn't want to anyway. The big issue, then, is to decide what data to collect and what not to. Once you've figured that out, you'll need to make sure that the data you do collect is the kind that will let you engage your customers in a lasting dialogue.

Gaining access to and integrating data from a variety of data-bases in your organization will be the single largest driver of the cost of implementing your email marketing programs. Therefore, it's going to be critical that you understand what data you need to sup-port your programs. Implementing your programs in phases will allow you to simplify the initial data you'll need to get your program off the ground, and will be key to a quick and successful program launch.

Data falls into two broad categories:

- *Aggregate data* is summary data containing such things as how many banner advertisements were served over a particular time, total number of clicks on links in an email or on a web page, how many web page impressions were served, which pages were most frequently viewed, how many inbound and outbound emails were received and sent, total number of products purchased, and so on. This type of data can help to ensure the overall success of your operations as well as give you some general insights into what your visitors and customers are interested in. But since it doesn't connect specific pieces of information to specific email recipients or site visitors, it alone is not particularly useful for email marketing.

- *Profile data* contains the individual history of every interaction that every customer has with you. While aggregate data deals with trends and generalities, profile data deals with specifics: specifically what individual site visitors are interested in, which emails they receive, which links they click on, and even what they purchase. This kind of data is what makes it possible to target and personalize email marketing programs.

For example, once N2K had implemented its opt-in email marketing program, MyMusicBoulevard, it began to analyze its customer purchase data. This gave it terrific insight into what its customers were doing. After the program had been operational for 90 days, N2K found that 32 percent of everyone who purchased at the site had signed up for the program. More important, these customers generated 40 percent more revenue per customer than nonparticipants in the program. Clearly MyMusicBoulevard had been successful in attracting the most valuable customer segments. While these (aggregate) statistics were crucial to demonstrating the success of its program, it was the ability to incorporate the information into each customer's profile that made it so powerful. The data was used to personalize communication with and service each individual customer.

N2K also learned that customers who made a second purchase within 30 days of their first were 50 percent more likely to buy a third time (and, possibly, a fourth, fifth, or sixth time) than those who didn't. This was a critical discovery. Immediately, one of the important goals of customer communication became providing incentives to customers to return to the site within 30 days of their first purchase.

Having a good handle on its profile data also enabled MusicBoulevard to react quickly when Frank Sinatra died in 1998. Within hours of the announcement of Sinatra's death, MusicBoulevard had secured exclusive online rights to the video of his life. It wanted to instantly deliver an email promoting this video to every customer who had purchased a Frank Sinatra CD in the past or who had ever indicated an interest in his genre of music. Every minute MusicBoulevard waited before getting these promotional announcements to its customers was a lost opportunity. Using profile data, however, MusicBoulevard was able to instantly begin communicating with a highly targeted group of potential customers and offer them a commemorative video.

DEVELOPING A CUSTOMER MODEL

Imagine that you're on your way to meet a blind date. There are probably a few things you'd like to know, right? You may, for instance, be interested in your prospective date's age, nationality, occupation, personal interests, religious orientation, favorite movies, books, and restaurants. Once you finally meet, of course, his or her appearance and clothing will give you some initial hints. And you'll get more clues when you actually talk—assuming, of course, that you speak the same language. Online meetings, though, provide far fewer cues than their real-life counterparts. Just because a customer you've just "met" online understands what you're saying doesn't mean that you're really communicating. You may think you're talking to an older man, for example, when you're actually dealing with a teenager, gen-xer, and so on.

If you're going to be able to truly recognize and get to know your customers, you'll need to develop a customer model that will enable you to target and personalize messages as well as to report on and analyze data. You simply can't get along without one. At its most fundamental level, a customer model is an abstract description of a customer, which you develop in order to support the business goals and objectives of your email marketing program. Your model will include any and all of the criteria you plan to use to select message recipients and tailor the content they receive, determine the proper contact sequence, and measure the results.

Data in the customer model (see the discussion of "source and types" of profile data later in this chapter) may be either raw or part of a complex model designed to track or predict customer behavior, measure customer value, etc. But you'll never be able to identify the precise information you need to implement and execute an effective email marketing program unless you have clearly defined your goals and objectives before you start.

This is exactly what eBags did even before it launched its website. It wanted to ensure that customer profiles would have enough information to enable eBags to engage each customer in every stage of his or her relationship with the company.

It was clear, then, that collecting detailed information from the very first contact with the customer would be critical if eBags was to achieve its business goals. It decided up front what information it would need to collect in order to immediately begin delivering value to its customers. By designing a comprehensive customer profile *before* it started collecting information, eBags has been able to assemble a large customer base, with which it's been engaging in regular dialogue since the site first launched. It doesn't need to go back to its customers and ask for additional information or for permission to send email because it's been doing so from the beginning. Furthermore, eBags has consistently listened to its customers and their feedback. As a result, even though the initial customer profile design was probably far from perfect, the company is still in a strong position because it knows exactly what works for it and what doesn't. The trust-based relationship it has been building with its customers has enabled eBags to involve its customers in the ongoing improvement of its site and to keep them engaged over time.

TYPES OF CUSTOMER PROFILE INFORMATION

Customer profile information can be classified into two general categories: *self-reported* (customers provide it to you themselves) and *observed* (you collect the information from other sources or you observe actual customer behavior). Whether profile data is self-reported or observed, be careful that you collect it from only the best sources. There are three basic qualities of profile data:

- *Good data* is guaranteed to be accurate, is kept secure and private, and is easily accessible (to customers) through active profiles that allow the customer to examine and update it. The more you can validate the sources of profile data, the more accurate that data will be. Data is "good" when you tell customers you're collecting it and they willingly give you permission to use it.
- *Bad data* is stale, out-of-date, or stored in such a way that consumers cannot examine or modify it.
- *Ugly data* has been acquired from unqualified, third-party, or otherwise unknown sources or is being used without the consumers' permission. Ugly data also includes information that is not being kept in accordance with local, state, federal, or foreign consumer privacy laws.

Harlequin Enterprises uses several sources of self-reported and observed information to build comprehensive customer profiles.

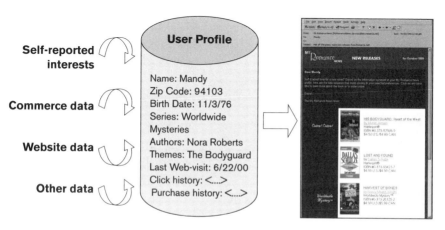

Data drives relevance.

"Self-Reported Interests" are collected from the sign-up form on the eHarlequin website. In programs such as these, "Commerce Data" is also often brought in from the e-commerce and catalog databases, "Website Data" is collected and supplied by the organizations or group hosting the website, and "Other Data" may include the data feeds from customer service, special contests, promotions, surveys, and so forth. All this information is collected with each customer's knowledge and permission in order to develop an email program that delivers relevant and timely offers, news, and entertainment.

DESIGNING THE CUSTOMER MODEL

As we look at the different sources of profile data, keep in mind that customer or member profiles are dynamic: they'll evolve as your relationship with the customer deepens. Your goal is *not* to collect all of this information at one time. Asking a lot of questions on a first encounter can be very off-putting. Imagine walking into a store and having someone come up to you, introduce herself as an employee, and immediately ask for your phone number and how much money you make. You'd probably react quite negatively and you might even leave. Asking for personal information on your website is no different.

The sections below outline some of the information you may want to include in your customer model. Data fields you may want to include in each customer's profile are included in angle brackets (< . . . >). Keep in mind that this information is valuable only if it supports well-defined business and marketing goals.

SELF-REPORTED PERSONAL INFORMATION

‹LAST NAME, FIRST NAME, EMAIL ADDRESS, CITY, STATE, ZIP/POSTAL CODE, GENDER, BIRTHDAY, PRIMARY LANGUAGE, OCCUPATION, MARITAL STATUS, NUMBER OF CHILDREN . . .›

Theoretically, all you really need to start communicating with an online customer is his or her email address. If that's all you have, though, all you'll be able to do is broadcast the same message to everyone. Always ask yourself the minimum amount of information you will need to begin your dialogue.

When developing customer profiles, leave it up to the customers to determine what they're comfortable sharing. Asking questions over a period of time is an effective way to show customers that you won't misuse the information they're sharing. Clearly indicating the value they'll receive in return can accomplish the same goal. Asking for the names and birthdays of a registrant's children may come across as invasive. But inviting a customer to sign up for a reminder and gift suggestion service for his friends and family (including, of course, his children) sounds a lot more innocuous and is more likely to get results.

In the case of eBags and its My eBags membership program, every program email delivers product recommendations and other content that is based on a member's chosen lifestyle interest(s). To ensure that every email remains personal, relevant and anticipated, the only personal information that eBags requires that you submit when joining the program is first name, last name, email address, lifestyle interest(s), email message type(s) you would like to receive, and a password to protect your file. Customers are asked for their full mailing address only when they make their first purchase.

SUBSCRIPTION INFORMATION

‹APPLICATION-DEPENDENT INTERESTS (MUSIC GENRES, FAVORITE ARTISTS, STOCK PORTFOLIO, TECHNICAL TOPICS, ETC.), DATE FIRST SUBSCRIBED, DATE OF LAST SUBSCRIPTION UPDATE, TYPE OF EMAIL PROGRAM, FREQUENCY OF CONTACT DESIRED (HOW FREQUENTLY THE CUSTOMER IS WILLING TO HEAR FROM YOU) . . .›

The most effective subscription forms are those that tie every question directly to the value delivered and make it clear which fields are required and which are optional. When you ask customers to list their favorite musicians, for example, tell them that you're asking so you can notify them when those artists release new albums. The online subscription form needs to be active at all times so that subscribers can easily examine and update the information. Be sure to ask consumers how often they want to hear from you. If you don't, you're risking overcommunicating with (and potentially alienating) them. When signing up for My eBags, a potential customer is required to answer only a few questions. Each question is designed to gather information that is clearly associated with lifestyle interests and is directly linked to the value a customer receives in return for signing up.

PURCHASE HISTORY

‹FIRST PURCHASE DATE, LAST PURCHASE DATE, PURCHASE FRE-QUENCY, PURCHASE VALUE (ACTUAL PURCHASES OR AVERAGE PUR-CHASE), PRODUCTS PURCHASED, PURCHASE DRIVER (WEBSITE "WALK-ON," EMAIL RESPONSE, BANNER CLICK-THROUGH . . .)›

Because past purchases are among the leading predictors of future interest, you should use the information contained in the customer's purchase history to determine the timing, offer, targeting, and personalization of your promotional communication. If, for example, you bought this book from BarnesandNoble.com, you've probably been identified as someone who's interested in high-tech business books, which means there's a good chance you'd be interested in Geoffrey Moore's *Inside the Tornado*. The level of detail you compile in your email marketing database is a function of the type of marketing programs you plan to execute. In many instances, getting a complete purchase history is overkill, and simple roll-ups indicating total spent by each customer, last purchase date, etc. will be enough. But if actual past purchases could be relevant to future communication, you need to keep, and take action on, this information. Modeling purchase behavior can help you predict possible future behavior. Identifying potential defectors, for example, gives you the opportunity to do whatever is necessary to retain them before they leave. (For more on this see "Modeled Information," below.)

EMAIL CONTACT AND RESPONSE HISTORY

‹EMAIL SENT, EMAIL BOUNCED, EMAIL OPENED, EMAIL CLICK-THROUGH, EMAIL CAPABILITIES (HTML, AOL, BROADBAND) . . .›

For a relationship marketing database to be successful it must include a complete history of all contact and interaction between you and your customers. This will, among other things, enable you to control the number of messages each customer receives, allow you to return to previously successful emails, and initiate follow-up communications with people who've received, responded to, or been successfully converted by those emails. For example, when eBags sends out emails—whether they're to My eBags nonpurchasing members or members who are also customers—it tracks all response activity. As a result, the company can identify not only which members have converted to customers but also which members are paying attention to the messages and staying engaged with the program regardless of their purchase activity. It then tests various offers and other email content to optimize sales and other program response levels.

WEB ACTIVITY

‹FIRST VISIT, LAST VISIT, DURATION OF VISITS, VISITS BY TOPIC . . .›

Until recently, most Web activity information has simply been used to inform the marketing and IT departments about how many page views, unique visitors, return visitors, etc., the website receives over a given period of time. Today, though, web marketers are showing increasing interest in integrating and leveraging customer-level website activity in marketing programs. Integrating web-tracking capabilities and your email program may, for instance, give you the capability to generate automatic email follow-ups when registered members or customers visit your site. Someone who spends a lot of time in the baseball section of a sports site could receive email featuring baseball more prominently than the other sports he might have expressed interest in when he registered.

eBags uses web activity reports to anticipate and predict interest among its prospects, members, and customers. For example, the company targeted its "Pack to School"™ promotion within online banner ads placed where it knew it would generate shoppers for its "Students" section, one of seven lifestyle categories within the eBags website. It not only prominently featured this "Make any purchase and get a free CD" offer across its website but, in particular, within its "Students" section, where users with the highest probability of responding to this offer would see it. In addition, My eBags members whose customer profiles indicated they had an interest in "Students" were targeted with email containing this promotional offer. As a result, this two-month promotion helped eBags sales jump 84 percent over the similar previous period; it also reaped a 2,663 percent ROI from this promotional event.

EXTERNAL ACTIVITY

‹CROSS-CHANNEL CONTACT HISTORY (MAIL, TELEPHONE), PENDING SUPPORT ISSUE, FIRST AND LAST SUPPORT CALL AND EMAIL, SUPPORT LOG/EVENT HISTORY, PRODUCT RETURN HISTORY . . .›

Data generated from your direct mail, telemarketing, customer support, and product return operations can be a critical part of measuring true customer value, cost to serve, and cost of customer contact and conversion. Linking this type of external data with your email marketing system will enable you to spot—and avoid— potential problems. Imagine, for example, that a customer has sent you an email complaining about a product defect. If customer service doesn't let marketing know about the problem, marketing might send the already-angry customer an email offering the latest add-on to the product he or she is complaining about.

Whenever eBags receives a customer service email, it triggers an automatic data feed to its email marketing system. This data feed places a "marker" in the customer's profile, which keeps the system from delivering any further emails to that customer until the marker has been removed (which happens only when the issue has been resolved).

EXTERNAL INFORMATION OVERLAYS

‹DEMOGRAPHIC INFORMATION OVERLAYS, PARTNER DATA OVERLAYS
(RETAILERS SHARING DATA AMONG THEMSELVES) . . .›

External information overlays are information acquired from outside sources that you add (or, as they say in the trade, "append") to your customer profiles. If you don't know what kind of cars your customers drive, for example, but you consider that information important, you can—in theory—acquire it from a third-party provider such as Axiom, whose large demographic database contains information on a majority of U.S. households. Information in overlay databases is normally collected from a variety of sources, some private and some public (such as your state's Department of Motor Vehicles or U.S. Postal Service change of address database).

Overlays are commonly used to enhance traditional direct marketing lists, but they are still fairly rare online. There are several reasons why this is so.

None of the commercially available services have email addresses for any significant portion of the consumers in their demographic database. This means that they cannot do an append keyed by email. You could use name and address as in offline direct mail, but many email marketing databases don't contain full name and address.

The usefulness of appends from traditional sources is still debatable. You might be able to improve the service you offer by using an append early on in your relationship with a prospective customer or member. In many instances, though, you'd be better off simply asking prospective consumers for the information you're looking for during the first online encounter. Most site visitors will tell you what kind of car they drive if they understand why you're asking and what value they'll get for answering. This gives you accurate, up-to-the-minute information instead of potentially old, and probably inaccurate, information.

Given the heightened sensitivity to privacy in the online environment, it's quite possible that appending customer profiles

with detailed demographic information could cause an out-
cry among consumer privacy watch groups and advocates.
While appended information from a third-party database may
improve targeting, it won't help with personalization. A database might, for example, reveal that 70 percent of your potential customers are women, but it can't say for sure which ones.
If you rely on that information you'll end up addressing a
number of men as Ms. when you send them email and that
won't do much to build their confidence and trust in you.

MODELED INFORMATION

‹DEMOGRAPHIC SEGMENTATION, BEHAVIORAL SEGMENTATIONS, LIFE-
TIME VALUE MODELS, PREDICTIVE MODELS . . .›

Developing analytic data models can help you understand many
of the less obvious aspects of your customers' interactions. This is the
learning part of the listening and learning we discussed earlier. Models are used to segment customers into groups with similar characteristics, behaviors, interests, and so on. They can be used to trigger
communication such as automatic win-back programs when the
model indicates that a particular customer is a possible defector.
Models enable you to design and develop new programs and campaigns based on your insight into your customers' behavior. (We discuss modeling and analysis techniques in greater detail in Chapter 8.)

MINING YOUR OWN BUSINESS

Most businesses collect a lot of information about their customers
that they never use. Big mistake. Instead of letting all those gigabytes
of customer information collect digital dust, use them to gain some
insight into who your customers are and how they buy. Doing some
data mining—exploring and analyzing the data you already have—
will give you a great head start on designing your email marketing
program.

N2K started its MyMusicBoulevard program by mining pre-
existing customer information. This helped it refine the design of its

subscription profiles to make sure it was collecting the right information from the start. Data mining also helped N2K expand beyond the Billboard Top 100 charts and offer MyMusicBoulevard subscribers a far broader—yet tailored—range of information and offers.

IDENTIFYING YOUR CUSTOMERS
BY THEIR EMAIL ADDRESSES

Having a unique identifier (UID) to identify a customer across multiple databases is an important—and frequently overlooked—concept. In the traditional world of direct marketing, a combination of name and address, and sometimes telephone number, is normally used to uniquely identify each customer. But because of the likelihood of misspelling names and transposing numbers, this approach is often less than accurate.

Because a customer generally remembers his own email address, that address can be linked with the UID in the database and used as a sign-on name for the customer, thus making it easier to maintain and track customer information over time. When designing a customer sign-on process, it's a good idea to suggest to users that they use their email address as their sign-on ID or user name. If you ask them to make up a user name, they'll quickly forget it. When this happens, the user will send you an email, call your 800 support number, reregister with a new user name, or disengage altogether, all of which costs you money.

A relatively small number of users share their email addresses with other members of their household, and this presents something of a challenge. To differentiate and support multiple members of a shared-address household, some customers may need to identify themselves through a combination of email address and user name, normally the user's first name. Whether you create customer profiles based on households or individual users will depend entirely on the objectives of your email marketing program, but in general, it's unlikely that you'll need to worry about this problem.

DOES EVERYTHING NEED TO BE IN ONE PLACE?

"To data warehouse or not to data warehouse" is a question that more and more companies are trying to answer. A data warehouse is a centralized collection of data. Its goal is normally to gather all the data that exists within your organization into one database, effectively becoming a central repository for data about customers, products, and transactions (potentially spanning all the company's divisions and products). The promise of a functioning data warehouse is phenomenal. It may enable you to put together a complete view of all customer activity in all channels. It should enable to you look at a history of product sales and cross-tabulate the sales history against customer information such as age, location, gender, or any other information that exists in the warehouse. Because no organization runs all its operations from a single database, the data warehouse also acts as a central clearinghouse, receiving and processing information from all the company's other databases and sending information out to them as well. As you may expect, building a data warehouse is a significant undertaking for any organization, small or large, but because of the scale of these projects, I have witnessed very few successful data warehouse initiatives. They always seem to be "under development" by the information technology department.

Does your organization need a data warehouse to develop an effective email marketing program? Not at all. A common mistake is for marketers to wait for the completion of a centralized data warehouse project before they move forward on data-driven marketing initiatives. I was recently speaking to a high-flying Internet start-up (which shall go unnamed) in the consumer retailing space. The company was very well capitalized, had aggressive plans to rapidly build a large customer base, and its initial focus was—as it should be—on new customer acquisition. We were discussing how to initiate an email marketing program that would support its acquisition program and enable it to establish an email-based dialogue with early customers and site visitors.

The marketing side of the business was very eager to get the ball rolling, but discussions broke down over the data warehouse effort.

The technical side of the business was convinced that it needed a data warehouse and that no email marketing programs should be developed until this effort was complete. This is a major mistake, one which I predicted would keep it from initiating an email marketing program for at least 18 months. In fact, its IT efforts so slowed it down that the company was months late launching its site, did just over $1 million in revenue, and then filed for bankrupcy protection.

A well-designed data warehouse can provide a rich source of data to draw from when developing your customer model, and it may expedite the development of a comprehensive, information-intensive email marketing program, but it is by no means a requirement. Building a data warehouse is a large, complex, and expensive undertaking. It is usually driven by the information technology side of a business and must support a broad range of departments other than marketing. Unfortunately, it is beyond the scope of this book to discuss the various types of commonly used data warehouse designs and architectures.

Data warehouses are also notorious for having all the right information but giving little or no practical or useful access to it. Most data warehouses, for example, are not designed to support real-time transactions and therefore will not provide the operational foundation for an integrated email marketing program.

THE EMAIL MARKETING DATA MART

Whether you decide to embark on a data warehouse project or not, if you're going to implement an email marketing program you will need to develop a data mart, which is a specialized database designed to support specific functions or applications. Data marts differ from data warehouses in that they are both special-purpose and transactional. They are *special-purpose* because they are designed to house only the data that is required to support the application they are being designed for. (In contrast, a data warehouse contains data for the entire corporation.) For instance, a marketing data mart will normally house data useful for understanding customer behavior. It will segment and target customers based on their demographic and self-reported profiles, past purchase history, and even elements of their customer service history. It will not contain such information as product specifications, shipping address, and credit card number. They are *transactional* because they are designed so the data can be used in real-time to drive such transactions as sending personalized email or generating detailed reports.

As was discussed earlier, the data that makes up the data mart is collected from any number of internal and external sources (possibly including the data warehouse). Having a well-designed data warehouse in place when you design and implement an email marketing data mart may make it easier to compile the information you need, but it's not at all necessary. An email marketing data mart can simply connect to a collection of databases—such as those used for registration, customer service, web-tracking, and commerce—to pull together the requisite information needed to support your email marketing programs. All the information in an email marketing data mart must be easily accessible and actionable, both for driving individualized email communication and for pulling reports in real-time.

ACCESSING CUSTOMER DATA IN A WORLD OF REAL-TIME EXPECTATIONS

If I register for an email service or make a purchase on a website I expect to receive a confirmation right away—and I'm not alone. Online consumers everywhere increasingly expect to receive immediate responses to their actions. Anything else is seen as a possible problem and could undermine my confidence in the company I'm interacting with. But in order to send out that instant welcome message or purchase confirmation, the marketer must receive the data—in real-time—on what I signed up for or purchased.

Consumers also expect to be able to examine and modify their personal profiles at any time. This means that the same data that drives email targeting and personalization must be available—again, in real-time—to the customer to whom it belongs. Customers expect that the changes they make to their profiles will take effect instantly. If I unsubscribe or change my address now, it isn't good enough that you update your database 24 hours later—especially if you deliver me an email reflecting my old profile in the meantime.

Just as consumers expect real-time action and reaction from the companies they communicate with online, marketers are demanding almost instant results from their email marketing efforts. Because 90 percent of responses to an email campaign typically come within 48 hours, it's very possible to get a sense of whether a campaign is going to work as expected within hours after the first emails are sent out.

Of course, not all data needs to be updated in real time. When you design your customer model it is important to consider what information really does need constant updating and what can be transferred into your email marketing database in batch mode at less frequent intervals. If you send out email from your marketing system only every night at midnight, there is no real reason to update the information in the marketing data mart more than once a day. But if you deliver all of your customer emails, including such real-time communications as purchase confirmations, through the same "communications gateway," the data indicating that a new purchase was made probably needs to be appended to a customer's profile within minutes of the purchase.

As time goes on, consumers and marketers alike will expect more and more of their transactional information to be available in real-time. Your challenge, then, is to keep your various data sources synchronized and updated in a way that supports your customers' expectations as well as your own communication needs.

PRIVACY, SECURITY, AND YOUR DATA

Because member and customer data are among the most valuable assets your company has, guaranteeing their security and integrity is critical. Customers want to be sure that information about their preferences and behavior will remain private and won't end up in the wrong hands. If you can't give your customers that assurance or control who has access to that data, you will severely undermine your customers' trust in you. Here are the steps you must follow to properly ensure the security and privacy of your customer data.

1. *Develop and post a clear and unambiguous privacy statement.* Tell your customers what data you collect about them and how you intend to use it. If you intend to sell or otherwise share the data you are gathering, let them know the circumstances under which their data might be sold or shared and how they can request that they be removed from your database or list.

2. *Develop corporate data-use and data-access policies and controls.* If a department or division within your organization builds an email marketing data mart and uploads the information to the corporate data warehouse every week, who has access to it and how will it be used? Can other parts of your organization download data from the warehouse and use it as they see fit? Establishing corporatewide policies for data use and information access is extremely important. That's why it's critical to define who "owns" a given database and what rights other internal constituents have to the data it contains. Breaches of internal company data use or data access policies can become a potential threat to data security.

3. *Perform regular, outside data-use audits.* Whether you build an in-house data mart for your email marketing programs or use a service provider to store and manage your customer data, you should perform formal audits to ensure that neither your company nor anyone else uses the data in ways that go against your policies. An independent data audit can be similar to a financial audit. In fact, several of the Big Six accounting firms have already established divisions that perform data-use and data-security audits.

4. *Schedule regular white-box and black-box security reviews.* Data security reviews help analyze the policies, procedures, and technologies your company has put in place to protect against unauthorized access to your customer data. A *white-box security review* evaluates access procedures and password change procedures, as well as the hardware and software protections used to secure your data. In a white-box review, the reviewers have access to all the information they need to analyze your security systems. A *black-box review,* however, is

more like a simulated hacker attack—an attempt to penetrate and compromise your data security by someone who has no knowledge of how your systems are actually configured.

5. *Don't include "access to money" in your marketing data mart.* Including "access to money" (i.e., credit card numbers) in your database instantly makes it a target for hackers. If you store this type of information, you'll need to take an extra series of security precautions such as building robust "fire walls." Information about what individual customers have purchased is very relevant and should be stored in a customer profile, but none of that information can be used to perform fraudulent transactions. There are very few reasons (if any) why your marketing data mart needs to contain direct access to money.

6. *Encrypt data transfers.* Encrypting any and all data that is transferred between your systems will ensure that "sniffers" (hacker types who eavesdrop on communications conducted over unsecured connections) won't be able to pick up any vital customer information.

7. *Determine and implement appropriate levels of security.* Security is not an absolute term, and different organizations will have different sensitivities to security issues. Some will invest heavily in expensive fire wall technology, while others will consider fairly simple access protection measures. If the data stored in your database is readily accessible and available through public venues, it's probably a waste of time and energy to design elaborate security measures to protect against unauthorized access. If, on the other hand, your data includes such customer information as email address, personal names and address, purchase history, and credit card numbers, it's a prime target for hackers and must be protected with a higher level of security, such as establishing a fire wall. Virtual Private Networks (VPN) is yet another security measure that can be used to create a secure (encrypted) network between two remote sites. This is often done to protect sensitive data when it's being transferred between sites.

Whether you've already made your first attempt to communicate with your customers online or are still in the planning stages, it's not too early to start gathering data and compiling your customer profiles. But remember: How much data you collect is not nearly as important as how good the data is. The information you incorporate in a customer profile will have a major impact on the type of programs you'll be able to implement and on whether those programs ultimately succeed or fail, so plan ahead and practice full disclosure with your customers from the very first encounter you have with each and every one. The earlier you know what information you need and the more openly you disclose to your customers what kind of data you collect and how you intend to use it, the sooner you'll be able to achieve the goals and objectives of your Internet direct marketing efforts, and the faster you'll start reaping the benefits of establishing relationships with your customers.

In this section of the book, we've discussed how important it is to think and plan strategically in order to develop successful Internet direct marketing programs. In the next section, we'll build on these strategic perspectives and get into the nuts and bolts of implementing an email marketing program.

PART III

IMPLEMENTING
CUSTOMER
DIALOGUE

CHAPTER 6

ESTABLISHING A FOUNDATION FOR INDIVIDUALIZED CUSTOMER COMMUNICATION

THE BEST EMAIL MARKETING PROGRAMS deliver very different messages to long-time customers than to first-time prospects. This may seem obvious and intuitive, but you'd be surprised how difficult it can be to implement.

It all starts with getting to know your customers. Simply put, you can never know them well enough. The more you know their interests, preferences, and personal profiles, the better you'll be able to deliver timely, relevant, and interesting information and offers. The more timely and interesting your information—in other words, the more value you provide—the more your customers or prospects will look forward to hearing from you. That all makes perfect sense, but what does "getting to know your customer" *really* mean? Let's take a look at a wonderful example.

N2K's MyMusicBoulevard (MMB) program encouraged users to sign up and tell the company a little about their musical interests and preferences. In exchange, MMB sent individually tailored, weekly emails with information on new releases from favorite artists, concert announcements, special deals, and industry news. A customer I know signed up for the program in the fall of 1998 and quickly began looking forward to his weekly emails. He actually *wanted* to buy a CD from MMB every week and was disappointed if a mailing didn't contain an offer or personalized recommendation that matched his interests. Price didn't matter (within reason). What did matter was convenience and assistance with his music selections. For the entire time he was signed up for MMB he didn't buy a single CD in a traditional retail store, nor did he make any purchases from other music-related web stores. And why should he? MMB knew him, they knew what he wanted, and they made it extremely convenient and fun to do business with them.

Giving your customers a structured forum for sharing their interests and listening to what they tell you is only part of the process of getting to know them. You also need to observe their behavior. As I've mentioned earlier, before N2K developed MMB it carefully analyzed six months of customer purchase behavior to determine which categories customers bought in, how often they bought, how much they spent, and when it had made their last purchase. This enabled the company to figure out what types of customers it had and helped it develop an effective contact strategy that would allow it to offer valuable, individualized services to each customer segment. (Please review Chapter 4 for the discussion about contact strategies.) This knowledge became the core of the MMB service. Once the service was launched, N2K was able to observe its new customers in order to promptly deliver relevant and timely communications. It was also able to identify potential defectors and use special, targeted offers and incentives to encourage them to stay.

BUILDING A RELATIONSHIP WITH YOUR BRAND THROUGH ONGOING COMMUNICATION

While you're building a relationship with your customers, who are they communicating with? Is it your CEO? Your VP of marketing? Is it the product team? Or is it the company itself? Actually, it's none of the above: Your customers are communicating with your *brand*. And as was discussed earlier establishing that relationship is a little like going out on a date. Imagine showing up for a first date and being handed a three-page form that asks for everything from your name, address, and income to your medical history and how many children you want to have. What are the chances that you'll want to go out with that person again? Pretty slim. But you'd be amazed at how many companies run their websites exactly like that. Instead of keeping the first date friendly and low-pressure, they drive potential customers away by asking all kinds of overly personal and seemingly irrelevant questions.

When striking up a relationship with a new customer or prospect, keep the following guidelines in mind:

- *You're not their best friend.* Nothing is worse than the used-car salesman type who pretends to be your best friend before he even knows your name.
- *Keep it short.* Don't go probing for all kinds of personal information right away. When asking questions, indicate why you are asking and what value your customer will get in return.
- *Listen.* Online customers expect to be in control, and if you listen, they'll tell you what they're interested in.
- *Deliver immediate value.* Start with a short email with some relevant information or a special offer.
- *Show them you heard.* Make sure that your follow-up contacts reference the information you received. This reminds your customers that you're actually using what they gave you. It builds trust and establishes permission for the next level of contact.

If you follow these simple guidelines for basic polite behavior, you'll quickly establish a solid foundation for a meaningful, committed customer relationship.

MANAGING THE CUSTOMER RELATIONSHIP CYCLE

Customer-company relationships go through a predictable four-stage cycle, and it's essential to keep your communication appropriate to the stage they're in. Let's take a look at these stages.

ATTENTION

You can't have much of a dialogue with someone if you can't get his attention. So you have a number of choices: You can be loud or friendly, or you can even try to buy his attention with money or prizes. As you consider your alternatives, think about the type of relationship you want your customers to develop with your brand. Do you want them to expect free gifts and special offers every time they hear from you, or do you want them to consider you a high-quality source of top-quality products and carefully considered advice and suggestions?

If you use sweepstakes or special promotions to attract prospective customers' attention you'll need to consider how those incentives impact your chances of engaging them further and taking them to the next level of the relationship. If a home supplies website is offering new registrants a chance at a free trip to Paris for two, are people signing up because they want two-by-fours or is it the prospect of eating crêpes on the Champs Elysées?

PERMISSION

Now that you've got their attention, you need their permission to move to the next level and begin communicating. This, in effect, is the actual "first date." Your goal during this stage of the relationship is to begin to convince your prospects that you are indeed the right brand for them to have a relationship with. You want them to opt in to the program or service you believe will provide them with convenience and value. Listening carefully at this point is critical. What are prospective customers looking for from you? How can you deliver service that makes them start thinking of you as a brand they would consider having a long-term relationship with? Go easy at this stage; a few questions are all you should expect them to answer.

INVOLVEMENT

When a customer makes a first purchase, she's showing that her interest in your brand is more than simply casual. She's gone from being a polite listener to being an engaged buyer. This is the point where you begin laying the foundation for a service relationship, which you'll do by delivering tangible value in the form of information, news, entertainment, and promotions that match your customer's interests.

LOYALTY

Moving from involvement to loyalty is like moving from a casual relationship to true commitment. Loyal customers or members are fully engaged. They are dependable, predictable, and valuable. They give you their business on a repeat basis and they're your avid and vocal advocates, telling their friends and colleagues about you at every opportunity. Your challenge, then, is to make sure your customers stay engaged with you.

A loyal customer has developed an emotional bond with your brand. The way to build loyalty is to continue doing what you did to get their commitment in the first place: Listen to what they tell you and respond with service and value. Once your customers begin buying from you, most likely they trust you enough to be comfortable sharing much more detailed information than they would have on your first date. Therefore you should gradually capture additional information that you can use to increase the level of individualized communication and service you offer.

ESTABLISHING INDIVIDUALIZED
CONTACT STREAMS

Now that we have the relationship life cycle down, let's see what it takes to develop truly individualized communication with thousands, or even millions, of customers.

FROM PERSONALIZED TO INDIVIDUALIZED CONTACT

Personalization and individualization sound as though they could be the same, but they're really quite different. Personalization includes things like addressing a customer by name and including items such as music reviews and special offers that are based on what the customer has told you and what you have observed about his or her browsing and purchasing patterns. Individualization, which supercedes personalization, goes much further by including a "strategic layer" that looks at each contact from a combined interest, lifestyle, timing, and event perspective.

To individualize contact you need to understand how each customer segment differs from the others and what each one's needs are. Within each segment you then drive contact based on where each individual customer is in his or her life cycle with your brand. You continuously track your interactions with your customers and prospects so that you can monitor their individual responses and react interactively, relevantly, and in real-time.

THE THREE DIMENSIONS OF INDIVIDUALIZED CUSTOMER CONTACT

Individualized customer contact is the function of three separate dimensions:

1. *Targeting.* Using data on your prospects' or customers' interests and actions, you can select subgroups of individuals who are "eligible" to receive a particular message or sequence of messages. A home gardening supply store, for example, may send a message to everyone who has bought a lawnmower from it in the last three months. It may refine the group to target only those who bought a particular model. Or it could target every customer who buys any kind of mower and automatically send a personalized thank-you note ten days after purchase.

2. *Personalization.* Once you've targeted the recipients of a message, you need to determine what the message will say and how you'll personalize it. You may choose to address the recipient by name: "Dear Bill." Or you may refer to something Bill has done: "Thank you for your recent purchase of our Turbo III Deluxe Lawn Mower." You may focus on something that Bill has asked for: "You have asked us to

notify you about new products we think might be of interest to you." You might even mention specific regional or seasonal events or attributes: "Fall is upon us, and time has come to begin to prepare for another winter of snow and ice."

3. *Timing and sequencing.* When should individual customers be contacted and how often? Events are leading indicators of a person's likelihood to respond. But the same events don't usually happen at the same time for everyone. Some, such as major holidays, are common to large groups of people. Others, such as purchases, birthdays, anniversaries, graduation, births, or moving to a new house are far more individual. Having bought a Turbo III Deluxe Lawn Mower ups the chances that I'll pay extra attention to news and information about gardening and landscaping. Since you know that I bought the model with all the special gardening features, you may want to notify me about the annual gardening show that's in town next week.

INDIVIDUALIZING CUSTOMER CONTACT

Table 6-1 presents a summary of the most common tools and techniques Internet marketers can use to communicate with their prospects and customers on an individualized basis.

Table 6-1 Tools for Individualized Customer Contact

Tools and Techniques	How They Help
Surveys: Ask a sample of your customers to tell you their opinions.	Although only a small percentage will participate, surveys can help you gain greater general insight into your customers' and prospects' opinions and attitudes. Appending survey data to customers' profiles can aid in follow-up communication and reporting. Online surveys can be performed quickly, gathering almost immediate results.

Tools and Techniques	How They Help
Self-reported interests: Use live profile pages and active subscription forms to capture each customer's interests and preferences.	These are core mechanisms for letting individual customers describe their personal interests and preferences, so that you can deliver relevant communications.
Web-tracking and profiling: Track known individuals' interactions with a website over time.	Knowing how often customers come to your store without actually identifying themselves has real value. So does knowing which parts of your site they spend most of their time on.
Purchase data integration: Integrate product (SKU)-level information about each customer.	Keeping track of customers' purchase history down to the product level tells you a lot about their wants and needs. You can use that knowledge to make highly relevant suggestions and recommendations and after relevant advice.
Global anonymous profiling: Anonymously track websurfers' actions across a network of websites.	You can know your customers a lot better if you can see what they do beyond the confines of your own store or website. While this technology has been successfully used to improve banner advertising efficiency, it will probably not be of much help building individualized customer dialogue for two reasons: (1) Data is anonymous and there is no mechanism for tying it back to individuals' profiles without raising severe privacy concerns; (2) there is no evidence that the level of information gathered by current anonymous tracking systems will be of significant value from a relationship management perspective.
Referral tracking: Keep track of who is spreading the word.	You can track when customers forward email they've received from you to a friend

Tools and Techniques	How They Help
	or colleague. You can even encourage them by offering incentives to do so. Knowing which of your customers are active e-community participants or sources of referrals can help you generate buzz and spread your message virally.
Customer service integration: Integrate individual customer profiles with a history of each customer's praise and complaints.	Keeping track of every issue—good or bad—that each customer has raised with you will effectively inform and generate future dialogue.
Modeling and analysis: Move from raw data to insight.	Just as the perfect butler always anticipates your next move, you must always stay two steps ahead of your customers if you're going to truly provide them with value. Analysis and modeling enable you to get to know your customers so well that you can predict their future behavior and anticipate their next moves.
Data overlays: Go outside to learn more about your customers.	By overlaying third-party data onto your own customer profiles, you can enhance each individual's profile with information you haven't been able to access any other way. The effectiveness of these programs depends on the quality and sources of the overlay data. Overlays may also involve some privacy issues.

THE CONTACT PLAN

CDNOW has to decide which of the 200 weekly new music releases to notify each of its customers about, who should receive its daily newsletter, and who is most likely to respond to its latest sales promotion. It uses a contact plan to help it narrow its choices and deliver the most relevant messages to its MyCDNOW members.

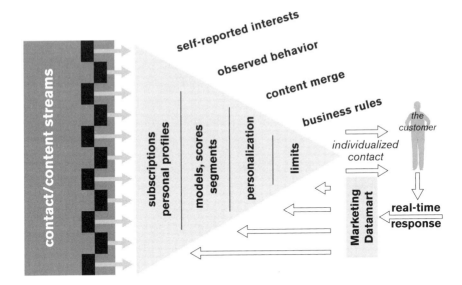

The contact plan.

Harlequin uses its own version of a contact plan to decide who should get its love horoscope or special announcements of authors hosting live online chats.

Narrowing a large number of contact opportunities down to an individualized contact stream can be a daunting prospect. To make it a little easier, though, we've developed a model called the "contact plan" (see figure), which helps answer the question of how to design and implement a contact plan that reflects every customer's unique needs and interests. On the left side of the contact plan is the input: all the possible contact opportunities. This includes educational and entertaining content, news, announcements, purchase confirmations, special offers, promotions, and more—in short, any email you might ever send to any customer. On the right side is the output: the individualized contacts that each prospect or customer will receive. The plan itself consists of five steps that systematically refine and customize contact on a large scale: *self-reported interests, observed behavior, content merge, business rules,* and *response (feedback).*

SELF-REPORTED INTERESTS

The value and importance of self-reported interests was discussed earlier in a general way. Let us examine how they work in a more detailed fashion. There are many different ways to provide a mechanism for members, prospects, or customers to tell you what they are interested in and, potentially, not interested in. The most valuable is to provide subscription or profile pages where they can sign up.

Understanding what information you need from a customer is critically important to successfully implementing an individualized contact plan. If, for example, you want to develop a birthday reminder and gift suggestion service for your customers, the most important information is the birthday of the person your customer is shopping for. How you ask the question is often as important as the question itself: Asking for the ages (in years) of all your customers' family members won't do you good; what you need is actual birth dates in month-day-year format.

Always allow your customers to engage with you one step at a time and to control what they receive from you and when they get it. We've discussed how this is key to developing their trust and confidence in your marketing efforts. By paying attention to what your members or customers tell you on their profile page, you will be able to narrow down the selection of what they receive by excluding all contact that doesn't map to their stated interest.

OBSERVED BEHAVIOR

Once you have received permission to contact your website visitors or customers, you need to start observing their behavior. This will help you intelligently select the content for each contact opportunity and limit those contacts to only the most relevant and valuable.

There are many different ways to observe and select customers and determine their value. The two most common are *response activity* (click-through) from your emails, which is a good way to gauge customers' general level of interest, and *purchase activity*, which provides a more accurate indication of interest and is a leading predictor of future customer value.

Another good approach is to measure customers' website activity on an individual basis. From an email marketing perspective it doesn't help much to know that 437,237 customers visited the sports section of your website last month. What can be very useful, though, is to know that Bob Smith visits the baseball section daily and looks at hockey scores once a week. If we were to send a personalized offer to Bob to buy season football or baseball tickets, it's obvious which one we'd lead with.

CONTENT MERGE

This is where we personalize the actual body of the message by fitting the appropriate promotions and content into the given contact opportunity so that the message will contain relevant and interesting information and offers.

One of the biggest challenges of trying to communicate with customers is that you may have more to say than opportunities to do so. For example, after processing your data through the first two stages of the funnel you see that a given customer might be interested in receiving five pieces of information. But you have a company policy of not sending more than two emails a week because your data shows that customers disengage if you contact them too often. The content-merging process will help you determine how to merge these five pieces into two separate contact opportunities. Perhaps you'll need to insert three personalized pieces in a newsletter and two more in a promotional announcement. This can be set up to occur automatically using personalization technologies or, in some instances, it may make more sense to define a manual process.

BUSINESS RULES

Your company's business rules define the criteria you use for message delivery, scheduling, prioritization, triggers, and limits. The amount of contact individual subscribers receive is driven by two factors: how much they want and the limits set in your contact plan. In some cases you'll ask your customers directly to specify the maximum number of emails they are willing to receive per week. In other cases you might be able to infer the answer from the programs they subscribe to. If, for example, a customer subscribes to your monthly newsletter and weekly promotions email but decides not to receive the daily announcements service, he is implicitly determining the number of emails he receives each month.

To maximize the relevance of each contact a customer receives you must establish a plan to prioritize what messages get delivered to each individual recipient. If you contact a certain customer segment only once a week, you want to make every message they receive count. To guarantee that your messages have maximum impact and generate the best responses, you must also control message delivery timing and coordinate delivery based on event-based triggers such as birthdays or anniversaries.

THE FEEDBACK LOOP

Once you make contact with your customers, you're going to start getting feedback from them immediately. And because everything is happening in real time, actions you take (such as follow-up messages) that are triggered by your customers' responses also have to be immediate. In this last, critical stage of the contact funnel you need to analyze customer responses and feed the results back into the data mart that is driving the funnel in the first place. Monitoring response patterns and refining and updating customer data will enable you to constantly improve the relevance—and the effectiveness—of every contact you make.

WEBSITES ARE STICKY; EMAIL IS ELASTIC

The term "stickiness" is used to describe how attached people become to a website and how often they use it. The most successful websites—certainly the ones that generate their revenue from banner advertising or purchase activity—are very sticky and get people to come back again and again.

So how does an organization build a sticky website? There are a lot of different ways. But what all the stickiest sites have in common is a focus on various aspects of the online service imperative. (As discussed in Chapter 1, these are service, convenience, and value). By offering free email to its members, portals such as Yahoo! and Excite encourage people to come back often. These "portals" also offer personal web pages such as MyYahoo! or MyExcite letting people check their stock portfolio, news, weather forecasts, and email—all without leaving their personal page. Online retailers such as CDNOW and 1-800Flowers update the content of their pages seasonally, weekly, and in some instances even daily. If you swing by the 1-800Flowers site around Mother's Day, there's little doubt about what you'll find. Perhaps not a site you'd visit daily. Rather, they've decided to create stickiness around the holidays and special events.

Online newspapers and magazines create stickiness by providing the latest news and entertainment. CNN.com would like your morning ritual to include a stop by its website to get a quick look at what's happening in the world. These sites have the latest news, hippest perspective, and hottest products—all tailored to you and your interests. When people visit a website where they know the content and offers are fresh and relevant, they want to spend time there. This, in turn, generates more click-revenue (ad exposure) for the site.

If the goal of a successful website is to be *sticky,* the role of successful email marketing is to be *elastic*—to reach out and pull people back. Although I love music, I only think about buying new CDs every once in a while. I'm not up to date on every week's new releases and I'm probably not going to go to my favorite online music store just to see whether anything I like came in. In other words, chances are pretty slim that I will visit an online music store very frequently. But email can change that. If I get a notice every week about what's new and exciting in the music genres I'm interested in, as well as personalized suggestions, I will be drawn right back in.

STICKINESS AND PERSONALIZATION

As I discussed above, MyYahoo! personalizes the service, news, and information I receive from Yahoo! I specify the stock quotes I want listed on my MyYahoo! page, I select the cities I want weather forecasts for, and I select categories of news I want to see. The best e-tailers are following suit and beginning to personalize their sites for individual customers. When you go to Amazon.com, for example, it displays and promotes books that relate to earlier purchases you have made.

What too many e-tailers fail to consider when planning to personalize their sites is that email can be very effective in accomplishing the same goals. Like a website, email can be personalized to contain content relevant to individual recipients. Email can also do some things that websites can't. Charles Schwab's website may help me track sudden changes in the price of a stock I'm following, but the information doesn't do me any good if it's only on my personal Schwab page and I don't happen to log on that day. But a timely, personalized email notification will almost certainly get me to visit the Schwab website to look into the matter further, and while I'm there, I might even make a trade. Email's elastic ability to reach out and pull me back greatly increases the stickiness of Schwab.com.

CAN CUSTOMER DIALOGUE BE AUTOMATED?

We've been talking about "customer dialogue" for several chapters, but we have never really formally defined the term. Let's do that now. As you might assume, "dialogue" implies a two-way exchange. An action is taken that is followed by a reaction, which in turn may generate a new action, and so forth. In some cases, the initial action may be an unsolicited visit to your website. The reaction in this case would be the display of your web page itself. Is your page static, with the same information displayed to every viewer, or do you generate a dynamic page that is customized when it recognizes the visitor, displaying appropriate content accordingly? In other cases, the action may be an email you send to a customer. The reaction would be the customer's response: sending back a reply or clicking through on a link in the message. Either of these reactions will in turn trigger another action by you.

Most marketing professionals will agree that the marketing discipline as a whole cannot be fully automated. But as we consider engaging thousands, perhaps even millions, of members, prospects, and customers in an ongoing dialogue, it's clear that at least *some* automation is required. So what can be automated and what needs the constant time and attention of human beings? And when is technology the answer to our problems and when does it make things worse? Table 6-2 shows some common *dialogues* that may occur between a marketer and a consumer and the extent to which the dialogue action and response is automated, manual, or both.

Table 6-2 Manual and Automated Email Dialogue

Dialogue Action:	Action Type: (A)utomated (M)anual	Dialogue Response:	Response Type: (A)utomated (M)anual
Consumer first visits website	(M)	Greeted as first-time visitor; invited to sign up for email newsletter	(A) (A)
Consumer signs up for newsletter	(M)	Personalized sign-up sequence; personalized welcome email	(A) (A)
Consumer returns to website	(M)	Greeted by name; presented with relevant content and/or promotions	(A) (A)
Marketer sends email notification	(A/M)	Open email; clicks on link	(M) (M)
Consumer makes purchase	(M)	Purchase confirmation email; automatic cross-sell email	(A) (A)
Marketer email promotion	(A/M)	Opens email; clicks to purchase	(M) (M)

Dialogue Action:	Action Type: (A)utomated (M)anual	Dialogue Response:	Response Type: (A)utomated (M)anual
Consumer sends customer service email	(M)	Confirmation email; automated email response; human email response; live chat response	(A) (A) (M) (M)
Marketer sends customer service email follow-up	(A/M)	Click-through to website	(M)
Marketer sends email newsletter	(A/M)	Opens email; clicks through for more information	(M) (M)

As you can see, most of the initial actions—whether they're initiated by the marketer or the consumer—are manual. Consumers don't usually have the ability to automate and generally have to manually initiate and respond to contact. At the same time, many marketing actions are driven by external and internal forces and events that cannot be planned for and therefore cannot be fully automated. Many of these actions also require creative and strategic input, which means that case-by-case planning is involved.

Responses to scheduled or predictable events, such as birthdays and purchase confirmations, can be automated by using database and personalization technologies, which will create highly personalized experiences for each customer.

THE 12 BEST PRACTICES OF SUCCESSFUL EMAIL RELATIONSHIP MARKETING

Intense competitive pressures, combined with easy electronic data flow and low-cost electronic communication, can too easily result in the mishandling of confidential customer data. The following 12 best practices can ensure that you will create a marketing culture based on full disclosure, integrity, and trust. Practices 1 to 5 deal with privacy issues. When customers know that the information they pass on to you is secure they will be more likely to share personal facts with you and you will have a better shot at keeping them engaged for the long haul. Practices 6 to 12 will help you build a community of valued and valuable customers—people who turn to you first, come back again and again, and bring others along as well.

1. *Develop and post a privacy policy.* Research shows that posting a privacy policy boosts response. Your privacy policy should include a comprehensive description of your trust-building practices and a clear statement of how customer information will and won't be used. To make sure your privacy policy is both visible and accessible, provide links to the policy page from your main website as well as from profile and survey pages and from the email you send to customers. Many customers will never read the policy at all, and almost no one will read it more than once or twice. But seeing it (or at least references to it) every time they have contact with you reassures them that you'll handle their information carefully and respectfully.

2. *Guarantee that each customer's personal information is secure.* Provide appropriate protection and security for your customers' profile pages. If confidential information is available on a customer's sign-up profile page, password protection may be appropriate. Explain to your customers when they enroll that password protection guarantees that they will be the only ones who will ever have access to their personal information. If your data and/or passwords are encrypted, you may also want to describe how this further enhances the security of a customer's personal information.

3. *Give customers full and easy access to their personal information.* Encourage your customers to actively manage their personal profiles, adding to or editing them any time. Build links to customer profile pages into your home page and your email marketing membership program pages. In every

message you send, invite customers, to review and update their profile. This reinforces their understanding that they always have control of their own personal information. As a result, they feel empowered to shape their relationship with you, and this will increase the quality of the information they provide.

4. *Account for any customer information you may already have.* When launching your email marketing program, you may choose to "pre-populate" membership enrollment forms with existing customer information. While doing this can save your customers time, it also risks making them uneasy if they don't know how you got the information that you have. To avoid this risk, describe where you got the information and encourage customers to edit the information. For example: "For your convenience, your customer profile page contains information you provided when you registered your product. Please review it carefully and make any changes you wish." The result? You save customers time while getting the most up-to-date information, voluntarily and directly.

5. *Never share customer information without permission.* Customers entrust you with information for a specific, stated purpose. If you wish to rent or otherwise share customer data, ask your customers' permission, allow them to refuse, and honor their wishes. Sharing customer data without permission can destroy the trust on which effective email marketing depends. Once lost, such trust is nearly impossible to restore.

6. *Link today's questions to tomorrow's value.* At the heart of email relationship marketing is the principle of fair exchange of value: customers provide information that's valuable to you in exchange for information, products, and/or services that are valuable to them. Gather only the information you need and explain exactly how you plan to use potentially sensitive information. For example: "Please provide your spouse's date of birth so that we can send you a gift reminder in time for her birthday." Over time you'll get

information and insight that wouldn't otherwise be available, and you'll end up with a powerful competitive tool to guide your business.

7. *Don't send unsolicited messages.* Contact only those customers who have expressed interest in receiving messages electronically and who have voluntarily supplied their email address. To guard against being perceived as a spammer, make sure your membership invitation explains to customers how you got their names and reminds them that they requested email contact. For example: "On your product registration form, you supplied your email address and asked that we contact you about product accessories." If a customer complains about unwanted contact, take action promptly: Offer an apology, unsubscribe the customer immediately, and provide the email address and/or telephone number of a senior marketing manager in case they wish to discuss the matter further.

8. *Enable voluntary completion of information.* Email relationship marketing depends on voluntary customer participation, so construct your sign-up (profile) pages carefully, making a field mandatory only when the information is truly essential for fulfilling a request. State for each question you ask why you want to know. For example, if a customer asks to be contacted by phone but omits a phone number, you might display a prompt such as: "You've asked us to call you when the product you requested is in stock. Please provide your telephone number so we can contact you promptly." Be careful, though. Soliciting information through mandatory fields often tempts customers to make up answers just to complete the form. If you explain how providing information will ultimately serve them, you increase their willingness to respond truthfully.

9. *Provide a fast, straightforward unsubscribe procedure.* Post this procedure prominently on your website and in all outgoing messages. Honor unsubscribe requests promptly (within 24 hours) and without fail. Making it easy to unsubscribe reduces the chance of antagonizing customers who

feel they're receiving messages against their will. A simple opt-out procedure also minimizes the risk that you'll be accused of spamming, a charge often leveled by people who want to get off a list but can't.

10. *Provide clear message subject lines.* Unlike traditional direct marketing strategies that often try to channel customers' attention toward offers, email marketing delivers a rich mix of communications tailored to known customer interests. Always write clear, descriptive subject lines for your customer communications: "Performance tip: Learn how to extend the battery life of your Palm V," or "Sneak preview: a new business tool to help you stay organized." More customers will read and respond to your messages, and your unsubscribe rates will stay low.

11. *Solicit customer feedback.* Email allows you to find out from your customers easily and directly what they think your company is doing right and where you can improve. Take full advantage of this opportunity by constantly inviting and encouraging customers to communicate with you. Here are just a few examples to consider: Establish an online suggestion box or message posting location on your website where customers can submit recommendations for new or enhanced products or services. Establish a dedicated email address so that customers can easily provide feedback on your email marketing program or other company practices. Acknowledge each message promptly, within 24 hours if possible. Assess the effectiveness of your program quarterly using customer satisfaction surveys. Don't just solicit feedback, do something about it. If you make a change based on something a customer tells you, say so. Customers who believe that you're listening to them will quickly become your advocates.

12. *Keep yourself honest.* Successful email marketing depends on doing what you say you're going to do. Invite an annual audit of your customer data-handling practices by a respected, trusted third party such as Price Waterhouse or TRUSTe. Build customer confidence by posting your compliance cer-

tification on your website. Monitoring and publicizing your compliance with privacy standards not only boosts customer trust and response rates, it can also earn your company a reputation as an active advocate of consumer privacy.

Every one of your customers is an individual and would probably like to be recognized as such. As we've seen, that's tough to do well. But after reading this chapter you now have a solid foundation for getting to know your customers. You know how—and why—to make ongoing communication an integral part of your relationships with your customers, you've got the tools to establish individualized customer dialogues, and you know the 12 best practices of email relationship marketing. In Chapter 7 you'll roll up your sleeves and start putting all the great ideas and concepts you've learned into action.

CHAPTER 7

KICKOFF: IMPLEMENTING
AND OPERATING A PROGRAM

WHETHER YOUR GOAL is to run a few simple test campaigns or to implement an advanced closed-loop email relationship marketing program, there are certain steps you'll need to follow. This chapter takes an in-depth look at the critical processes and procedures for collecting customer data, staffing, building a data mart, and even making a decision about whether or not to outsource any of these functions. We'll also learn how to design and generate the email that actually goes out to your customers as well as how to produce and analyze reports about customer usage. There's a lot to cover, so let's get started.

THREE WORDS THAT SPELL SUCCESS:
CRAWL, WALK, RUN

One of the most common mistakes companies make in the early stages of implementing their customer engagement strategy is to be overly ambitious. Having a vision, of course, is wonderful and I encourage every company to articulate a bold vision, but it's very important to set realistic and achievable goals. The advice I usually give companies is to learn to crawl, then to walk, then to run.

Implementing a fully integrated, best-practices email marketing program is a significant commitment. But by easing into it you'll be able to run some tests and demonstrate the program's value before you need to get a lot of people from different departments to sign off on it. Once you can demonstrate the program's value in real, quantifiable terms, you'll find it a lot easier to gain the support you need to expand the program's scope and capabilities.

Building a fully integrated customer communication program that will engage your prospects and customers in a lasting dialogue is like training for a marathon: you have to start slowly, gradually building up your strength and endurance. But unlike running the marathon, building a successful communication program is truly a team effort. If any one member of the team is not fully prepared and committed, the whole effort will suffer.

ASK AND YOU SHALL RECEIVE: COLLECTING EMAIL ADDRESSES AT ALL POINTS OF CUSTOMER CONTACT

Every time your organization is in contact with customers—whether they're making a purchase from your retail store, website, or catalog or simply calling your support line—ask for an email address. Because email addresses are unique, they are a better way to identify and track people than mailing addresses, phone numbers, or even last names, all of which can be accidentally duplicated or transposed. An additional advantage of asking for email addresses in, for example, your retail stores, is that it reinforces the idea in your customers' minds that you want to stay in touch with them. It also reinforces the idea that you're an Internet-oriented company. This can be a powerful way to support your brand image.

Using an email address as a unique customer key also makes it easy to measure customers' cross-channel behavior. Collecting email addresses at your points-of-sale, for example, serves a dual purpose: First, if you run an email campaign encouraging customers to visit your retail stores, you will measure how much additional traffic the campaign generates. Second, it gives you a way to reach out and communicate with new customers. The fashion footwear retailer Nine West encourages customers to submit their email addresses—

whether they're shopping through the catalog, in a retail store, or on the Web. The company developed an email program called Club Nine, which delivers periodic emails with news and sale notifications to customers.

Unfortunately, most existing point-of-sale and customer service systems aren't designed to house email addresses, and the challenge of including them in the customer record can be significant. Nevertheless, there is no reason why you can't update your systems to include this vital information—it all depends on your priorities. And while you're waiting for your information technology department to update your systems and databases, you can still do things the old-fashioned way. Just collect the email address on paper registration cards. Then manually key them into a database with feeds to your email marketing system. This is precisely what Nine West did.

HELPING YOUR CUSTOMERS SUBSCRIBE

A seemingly obvious but much-ignored point is to ensure that you make it easy for prospects and customers to sign up with your company. Don't make a visitor to your website have to search to find out how they can receive more information from you. Every home page should have a "Keep Me Posted" field where visitors can enter their email addresses. In some instances it may make sense to offer an incentive to get people to sign up, but if they're signing up to receive a valuable service, you won't need to. In many cases, when visitors enter their email addresses and click "Submit," they're taken to an additional profile page that asks a few more (optional) questions. You already have their email addresses, so if they don't answer the questions, you can reach out and try to reengage them. If they do answer the questions, you'll be better able to understand their interests, which will make it possible to instantly deliver value in your follow-up emails. The clearer you are about what you offer if someone signs up, the better your results will be.

A health and beauty products retailer who has successfully been using personalized email newsletters to follow up with its online customers, recently decided to sink $25 million into a television advertising campaign designed to increase brand awareness (and, naturally, to generate sales). The ads were extremely well done and drove a lot of traffic to the site. What the company hadn't fully considered was that, once on the site, most people wouldn't buy anything on their first visit. To make things worse, the initial newsletter program was tied to setting up an account with the retailer and required a fair amount of information that most first-time visitors simply weren't comfortable sharing. In addition, the sign-up button was a barely visible link near the bottom part of the home page. As a result, if visitors didn't buy on their first visit, they were probably lost forever. There was no simple way for someone with a passing interest in what the company had to offer to identify herself and ask for more information.

The website team had done what it is so easy to do when you work on something every day: They had lost their objectivity and hadn't realized how difficult it would be for first-time visitors to figure out how to actually register for the newsletter and the other cool, service-oriented information. To remedy the situation, they placed a "Get Connected" button prominently on the first page, and promised "promotional discounts and special offers" for signing up. All that was required was an email address. Two weeks after the new sign-up process went live, they had 6,000 new subscribers. Needless to say the Get Connected button still remains on the site.

Another online service provider saw its sign-up for email plummet as a result of a site redesign. Originally, the sign-up appeared prominently on a relatively uncluttered home page. The company beefed up the home page and in the process dropped the email registration to the bottom left-hand corner. As a result, the percentage of site visitors who signed up immediately dropped from about 9 percent to about 4.5 percent.

By making it very easy to sign up a first-time visitor or customer and then follow up later with additional questions, you're encouraging them to get engaged with you gradually as they discover the value you provide. Remember MyPlay.com, your private online music locker that we talked about in Chapter 1? A few days after new members sign up and have a chance to get a taste of MyPlay's benefits, they receive an invitation to set their preferences. They're invited back to describe the subscriptions they want, their experience level, digital music interests, and how often they'd like to hear from MyPlay. Members are in full control of the communication flow.

HELPING CUSTOMERS UNSUBSCRIBE OR MODIFY THEIR PROFILES

Although it's pretty obvious that you want to make it easy for visitors to subscribe, it's almost counterintuitive to want to make it easy for them to unsubscribe. In fact, as strange as it sounds, unsubscribe processes and procedures are an important component of the "listening" part of your dialogue with your customers. If a customer tells you he no longer wants to be engaged with you, what does he really mean? Does he dislike your product or service? Did you send him too many emails? Is the content you're sending him boring and unengaging?

If someone truly does not want to hear from you, don't waste your precious marketing dollars trying to change his mind. But if he's willing to stay engaged if you provide more value, you must make it clear that you can do so only if he gives you more specific information about what he really wants. And remember: Just because people choose to unsubscribe doesn't mean that they won't continue to purchase from you or use your services.

On average, between unsubscribers and dead (inactive) email addresses, most online retailers lose the ability to communicate with 2 to 4 percent of their customers every month. Since it's so easy to get free email services through Yahoo! and Hotmail, people who sign up just change their address if they start getting spam or too much email. For that reason, rapid changes in unsubscribes or dead email can sometimes be an indicator that you're overcommunicating with your customers. You should, of course, investigate anything above the 2 to 4 percent figure—and anything much below it too; it could mean that you've made it too difficult for customers to opt out of your campaigns. This often leads to high levels of pent-up dissatisfaction, which means that spam complaints are probably just around the corner.

One leading online retailer was very hesitant to implement one-click unsubscribe, thinking that it would lose subscriptions if it made it too easy for customers to disengage. But after implementing this feature, it actually discovered that its subscription base *increased* faster than before. People were responding to the fact that they were given complete control.

As this example illustrates, a well-designed unsubscribe process can greatly increase your email marketing program's overall effectiveness. The best ones are modular, meaning that they're designed to allow participants to interact with the program and modify their profiles to reflect their current interests. If the only option dissatisfied customers or subscribers have is to unsubscribe completely, that's what they'll do—and you'll lose the ability to stay in contact. If, on the other hand, you make it extremely easy to modify or update a subscription, a greater percentage of subscribers will stick with you. ShopperConnection (www.shopperconnection.com) is a consortion of top-tier retailers operating a website service that lets consumers sign up to receive a promotional newsletter from a network of 15 e-retailers such as Garden.com, CDNOW, and Reel.com. The newsletter consists of special offers from each of the retailers that the ShopperConnection member opted to receive information from. When new members first sign up to receive the newsletter, all they need to do is submit their email address. Selecting individual retailers is optional—the default being that every new member receives information from all of them. But in every email subscribers can modify their profiles by selectively removing retailers they don't have an interest in hearing from as well as adjust the frequency with which they receive the newsletter.

Having a good unsubscribe policy in place does not guarantee that you'll be problem-free. Despite your best intentions, data and technology are frequent sources of problems. When CDNOW and N2K merged there were some overlapping customer records. In addition, both companies had allowed customers to create more than one account. Not surprisingly, the merged CDNOW-N2K database contained multiple records—many of which had different email addresses—for a number of customers. As a result, some customers who began receiving multiple copies of the same email got overwhelmed and wanted to unsubscribe altogether. But even after unsubscribing from one account, many continued to receive emails through their other email account(s). Some customers concluded that CDNOW wasn't honoring their request to be removed. It didn't take long for a few of these irate customers to post stories that CDNOW was refusing to remove them from the email program. Soon, accusations of spamming began to surface, and customers' trust in CDNOW began to suffer. Meanwhile, behind the scenes, CDNOW spent significant resources remedying the problem, frantically trying to locate the multiple account "victims" and communicate with its customers in accordance with their stated preferences.

Here are some of the things you can do to minimize your chances of experiencing this kind of problem.

STRONGLY ENCOURAGE ONE ACCOUNT PER CUSTOMER

Whether customers buy from you or subscribe to your email service, accessing their existing subscription profiles or account information must be easier than creating a new one on every visit. Duplicate records can result in multiple messages to your customers and can make it very difficult to keep track of them as individuals. This can complicate your efforts to understand basic customer behavior patterns such as repeat purchases.

PROVIDE ACTIVE, USER-MODIFIABLE PROFILES

Subscription profiles and account information must always be active so customers can review, update, or remove their personal information. For instance, one-click-modify is a powerful tool for engaging your customers in dialogue. By encouraging them to click through to their personal profile page, you're asking them to come back and tell you what they like and what they don't. An active profile page should give customers access to all the data that you have on them, including name, address, email address, stated preferences, and how often they want to receive email from you. If the process of updating or modifying a profile isn't simple and intuitive, your subscribers will simply unsubscribe.

ENABLE USERS TO MODIFY THEIR PROFILES
DIRECTLY FROM WITHIN AN EMAIL

HTML email lets you ask profile questions from within an email just as you would on a web page. For example, newsletter subscribers might selectively unsubscribe from individual elements of the newsletter by clicking on a link in the letter itself. Subscribers would still receive the newsletter, but it would contain only those features they want to see.

Another approach is to use email to ask questions about a new functionality you may be offering and allow customers to sign up for it directly from within the email. If Petopia was introducing a new pet birthday reminder service, for example, it might choose to invite recipients of the *Petopia Post* email newsletter who had not already provided essential pet information to sign up by entering their pet's name and birth date in an online form. This information would automatically be appended to the owner's profile, and Petopia would be able to send birthday reminders and gift suggestions at just the right time.

DEVELOP EMAIL PROGRAMS AROUND
INDEPENDENT SUBSCRIPTION CHANNELS

Channels can be organized around topics, themes, products, services, or even frequency of contact. You may also choose to organize your email marketing program's different offerings along these lines. Let's say WineShopper.com wants to send its members a mixture of emails containing wine reviews, special deals, and notifications of tastings and events. If WineShopper.com chose to organize by channel, customers would be able to sign up for the Wine Review Channel, the Special Deals Channel, and the Events channel. What's nice about organizing your email marketing programs this way is that the word "channel" clearly communicates the idea that you can turn one on or off without touching the others.

INTEGRATE UNSUBSCRIBE CAPABILITIES
AT ALL CUSTOMER CONTACT POINTS

Imagine that you receive regular emails from E*TRADE® about your portfolio, new product announcements, etc. You have both work and home email addresses and would like to update your profile so that you receive your email at home instead of work. Perhaps you remember that you want to make the change while you're driving to work and call E*TRADE® from your cell phone. Maybe you send it an email asking it to make the change, or maybe you simply pull up your profile and make the change yourself on the website. Either way, E*TRADE® must enable its customers to easily update their personal profile.

A fully engaged organization will allow customers to update their profiles via email, website, or phone, at one of its retail outlets, or at any other contact point.

RESPOND QUICKLY TO UNSUBSCRIBE REQUESTS

Users who reply to an email from your company and put the word "unsubscribe" in the Subject field should automatically be removed from that email program. In addition, every email you send out should remind recipients that they can also unsubscribe online by clicking on the link that takes them straight to their Web profile form. When a subscriber lets you know he doesn't want to receive certain types of information from you anymore, honor that request immediately. If you send out emails every day, you must process unsubscribe requests within hours after receiving them to minimize the risk that customers will continue to receive mail after they have unsubscribed. If, on the other hand, you send monthly emails, updating your database once a day is often enough. Because unsubscribe requests can be performed on a batch basis, problems may arise due to updating, transferring, and synchronizing data among various databases such as the customer service, the website, and the email database.

LISTEN TO AND LEARN FROM YOUR UNSUBSCRIBERS

Constantly evaluating why your customers choose to modify their profiles or disengage entirely is very important to the ongoing success of your program. Is there a correlation between unsubscriptions and the timing of your mailings? Is there a correlation between unsubscriptions and the volume of email individual recipients receive? Is there a certain point in the customer life cycle where customers tend to unsubscribe? Do groups of unsubscribers share any noticeable characteristics (age, gender, etc.)? To find out what factors are influencing your customers' behavior, you may want to perform surveys, test different contact strategies, or vary your message frequency. Imagine a sporting goods retailer who is sending its customers email containing syndicated articles, information, and promotions. Sometime in May or June the company notices that it has abnormally high unsubscribe rates. Upon investigation it realizes that the people who signed up for the Winter Sports channel are unsubscribing at twice the usual rate. The reason becomes obvious: People aren't all that interested in winter sports in the spring and summer months, but the email program kept delivering weekly emails with updates and the sale notifications. By recognizing the seasonal nature of the relationship it has with this segment and reducing its email volume during the spring and summer months, the retailer could occasionally stay in touch with its customers but not bother them with irrelevant information. When fall rolls around, the company can up the email volume again and begin generating new interest and excitement. The lesson is this: If you listen to your customers, they'll tell you exactly how to make your email marketing programs meet their expectations. And this will ensure that they stay engaged.

ESTABLISH POLICIES AND PROCEDURES FOR DEALING WITH COMPLAINTS

No matter how well you follow all the best practices for email marketing (see Chapter 6 for a review) or how careful you are about asking permission before making contact, sooner or later you're going to get some complaints. Don't ignore these complaints; otherwise, they can quickly become a liability. If you've designed your program well, you'll have established clear processes and procedures for understanding, categorizing, managing, and responding to complaints.

Be absolutely sure to handle every complaint promptly and honestly. Here's what happened to an online promotions company which we'll call PromoCorp. PromoCorp had been working with an outside service provider to deliver its email promotions as well as to implement and maintain an unsubscribe process. In 1999, Promo-Corp switched to a new email marketing service provider. When the new provider delivered the first emails on behalf of its new client, a few *very* irate people instantly responded, saying that they had asked to be removed from the program a number of times and that they had the emails to prove it. One of the most vocal actually reported PromoCorp and its service provider to the Real-Time Black-Hole List (RBL), an anti-spam list that a number of ISPs subscribe to. Anyone sending mail from an address listed on the RBL is instantly blocked by all the other ISPs subscribing to the list.

PromoCorp's new service provider spent close to two weeks and countless staff hours trying to untangle the RBL problem. Eventually it discovered that the reason unsubscribed people were still receiving emails was that PromoCorp had not properly maintained the original membership data and that the company hadn't adequately defined procedures for handling problems and complaints. But the damage had already been done. Thanks to one individual, coupled with poor data-handling procedures, PromoCorp was blocked from reaching nearly 10 percent of its customer base by email for several weeks!

You absolutely must establish processes for quickly resolving issues like the ones described above. If you decide to implement and operate your own email marketing system, you must forge relationships between your company and the various privacy and special interest groups, such as the RBL. If you choose to work with a service provider, make sure it has established these relationships.

You must also consider how to respond to people who complain. If they're upset because they feel you're sending them stuff they didn't sign up to receive, do you send them yet another email letting them know that you've removed their name from the program, or do you just remove them and say nothing? In almost all cases you're better off promptly unsubscribing the person and following up with a very brief confirmation and apology for any inconvenience. Here's an example:

> *To: "B. Smith" <bsmith@somenetaddress.com>,*
> *<postmaster@MYCOMPANY.COM>*
> *From: "John R. Ellis" <ellis@MYCOMPANY.COM>*
> *Subject: RE: Holiday Gift Offer from MYCOMPANY.COM*
> *Cc: <abuse@prserv.net>, <abuse@wcom.net>, <abuse;@MY COMPANY.COM>*
>
> *Dear Mr. Smith,*
> *I have unsubscribed you from MYCOMPANY's email program.*
>
> *MYCOMPANY takes the issue of spam very seriously and does not intentionally send unsolicited email. Our contractual privacy policies can be viewed at www.MYCOMPANY.com/privacy.html.*
>
> *On behalf of MYCOMPANY, I apologize for the inconvenience and annoyance. If you have any further issues, please do not hesitate to contact me personally.*
> *Sincerely,*
> *John R. Ellis*
> *VP/Dir., Customer Marketing*
> *(415) 555–3036*

When Palm Inc. first launched its InSync Online program, it sent out email invitations to several hundred thousand customers who had registered their handheld computers by filling out a traditional paper registration card. The cards included a request for an email address as well as a box that registrants could check if they did not want Palm to send them emails. (Naturally, people who didn't want any mailings could have just as easily left their address off the card.) Those who checked this box didn't get an invitation to participate in the InSync Online program. Despite these precautions, a few people, claiming they had checked the opt-out box, received invitations anyway and immediately accused Palm of spamming them.

Palm looked up each of these people in its database to see whether it had made an error. It found out that the people complaining had actually *not* checked the "Please don't send me email" box. Nevertheless, Palm sent each one a personal email, signed by the director of marketing for the InSync Online program. The note explained why Palm had sent the email, apologized for the inconvenience it may have caused the recipient, promised no further emails from Palm, and included a direct telephone number to the director of marketing if the recipient of the email wanted to discuss the matter further. Including a phone number instead of an email address was a deliberate choice: It's a lot easier for an irate customer to mouth off in an email than on the telephone. And with email, a lot more people can find out about the complaint and jump on the bandwagon. Palm's clearly defined procedure for handling these kinds of complaints involved direct human intervention at an early stage.

There are, of course, some small, hard-core groups on the Internet who believe that almost any email of a commercial nature qualifies as spam. It's best not to get into a debate with these people; simply remove their names immediately. This real-life example between an online retailer and someone who had been receiving its email, illustrates how people can get very upset very quickly when their requests are ignored.

A. Jones wrote on 07:46 AM 11/18/99-0800—

I am getting DAMNED TIRED of telling MYCOMPANY to stop sending me junk e-mail.

This is my third message replying to this unwanted Internet abuse. Stop sending me unsolicited commercial e-mail (SPAM). Any further such occurrence will result in legal action for harassment, theft of computer services, and violation of federal and state telecommunication laws including anti-SPAM ordinances.

Service provider: This message especially applies to you as the California-based firm originating and directly in violation of CA's new anti-SPAM law. Cease and desist or face prosecution.

A. Jones

Determining when to respond with an apology and explanation and when to quietly unsubscribe a person is a case-by-case decision. In some cases you may be able to deal with complaints even before an angry customer contacts you. People often write complaints to threaded discussion groups in an online forum. If the issue is a common one, an escalating conversation can quickly develop. By monitoring these types of forums, you may be able to proactively nip potential problems in the bud.

STAFFING AND RESOURCE PLANNING

No two companies will have the same staffing requirements for their email-based customer marketing and communications programs. Your staffing will depend on the objectives and scope of your programs and whether you choose to build your own email marketing capabilities in-house or outsource them. Even if you outsource the system and technology operations, you may, for instance, choose to keep your strategic program planning, program design, or certain campaign execution functions in-house.

Because of the infinite number of ways to engage your customers, it's not possible to give a generic overview of how any particular program should be staffed and organized. Let's take a look at some important positions that you may need to fill to implement and operate your strategic email marketing program.

> *Relationship marketing manager.* The first person you need to hire is your program's designated "owner," the person who will ultimately be responsible for the success or failure of the entire initiative. This person may come from your e-commerce effort, your IT group, or even your customer service department. As the title implies, the relationship marketing manager is responsible for managing the relationships between your company (the brand) and your prospects and customers. This senior staff person will commonly be in charge of a broad range of your online relationship marketing functions, but his or her focus will often be on the email marketing program, as this communications effort is a pillar of

any greater relationship marketing and management function. The relationship marketing manager must be adept at coordinating programs among different parts of an organization as well as with external service organizations, and must own the vision of how your company develops long-term, loyal relationships with its customers.

Email marketing manager. The email marketing manager usually has a background in direct or relationship marketing as well as online marketing. The job requires someone who can work closely with both internal resources (including creative services, product groups and IT) and external service organizations to manage the email marketing program. The email marketing manager will also be responsible for the day-to-day operations of the program.

Marketing strategist. A marketing strategist works closely with the relationship marketing manager, the email marketing manager, and the data analyst. His or her job is to ensure that the program has well-defined strategic goals and that it isn't just a tactical tool for sending out large volumes of indiscriminate emails. The marketing strategist is responsible for coordinating with the broader marketing teams as well as the email marketing team to continuously test, evaluate, and optimize program performance to drive increased customer value. In some instances the marketing strategist and email marketing manager positions can be combined into one.

Data analyst. Your data analyst will use sophisticated modeling tools to analyze the data you are continuously collecting about your prospects and customers. These analyses will give you a better understanding of which parts of your contact strategy are working and which aren't. Working with the marketing strategist, the data analyst can help define data collection requirements, develop customer models, and design the customer profile data.

Creative producer. An email marketing program needs ongoing creative design and production resources. The creative producer manages the creative process, including coordinating graphic designers and copy writers.

Graphic designer. Very few (if any) programs rely simply on plain-text email. Sophisticated graphics, including text layout, images, animation, audio, and even video can be incorporated into email marketing programs. Because there are a number of technical constraints imposed on graphics in email, try to hire someone who has actual experience designing and producing graphics for email.

Copy writer. Writing copy for email is different than writing for advertising, direct mail, or even a website. Email copy should be brief and make active use of links that lead readers to more information about what they are reading about. How your copy is written can have a big impact on the overall campaign's performance.

Program manager. The program manager handles the day-to-day management of the message production process and is responsible for loading messages into the marketing system, scheduling message delivery, coordinating technical changes to message and personalization templates and data, and testing messages properly before they are delivered.

Technical manager. Depending on the complexity of an email marketing program, you may need a technical manager to oversee its implementation and ongoing operations. The technical manager manages any customized programming and database work that's necessary to implement a program.

Technical liaison. This person must understand technology and be firmly grounded in marketing as well. Responsibilities include bridging the gap between your marketing and technical teams. The person in charge of technical liaison works to facilitate communication between the marketing teams and the technology teams, hashing out issues, and keeping efforts synchronized and expectations aligned.

Application engineer. Once your program is actually up and running, you probably won't need full-time engineers. But depending on the program's size and scope, you may need to employ one or more engineers during the initial setup and whenever you need to make changes to the program. Engineers are responsible for any programming (of which there is often a fair amount) required to customize an application.

Database administrator. Your database is central to your email efforts. The database administrator will be responsible for ensuring that the database is at maximum performance level, that backups are being performed routinely, and that data imports and exports are seamless.

System administrator. The system administrator is responsible for administering all the hardware and software involved in operating the email marketing technology infrastructure. In addition to the database, this may include actual message generation and delivery, tracking, maintaining customer profile pages and Web-based applications that marketers use to plan, target, schedule, test messages, and so forth.

Quality assurance tester. To assure that every email message delivered is of the highest quality, you need testers. The tester is responsible for all aspects of your program relating to its quality and performance. Note that the quality assurance testing function is designed to assure that no Web links or personalization scripts are broken, that the message looks good in all formats, and so on. The tester is not responsible for testing the effectiveness and success of your overall marketing program.

SEEKING THE SOURCE OF KNOWLEDGE: ACCESSING THE RIGHT DATA

Difficulties accessing data are the most common causes of increased costs and program delays, so if you're going to design and operate a successful email marketing program, the data you use to drive the program must be readily accessible or actionable. Companies often keep data in a multitude of databases of varying quality. Here are the steps you need to take to successfully locate and access your data.

1. *Understand your data needs.* Develop a schedule for your data needs. Most likely you won't need everything when you first launch, but later you will need additional data to support more advanced operations. Describe the dependencies

among desired features and functionalities and the supporting data. When Petopia.com first launched its email marketing program, the Petopia team knew it wouldn't need pets' birthdays right away, but it had plans to use this information later. Petopia got the program up and running quickly by simplifying the initial data designs to include the most basic information, such as email address, name, and type of pet. Within six months of program launch, it had begun to collect additional information so that it could launch an automated pet birthday reminder service.

2. *Perform a data audit.* Develop a data map that shows where all relevant data resides and how it can be accessed. What data already exists? How frequently is it updated? What is the quality? Does it need to be consolidated from multiple sources? Is there a lot of duplication? OfficeMax collects information about customers online, through its catalog and telephone operations, and in retail stores. When the company first began planning its email marketing program, it needed to do a comprehensive data audit across all these points of contact. Although some data was being gathered into a central customer database, it was not clear what other customer information might exist that could be useful for the email communications programs.

3. *Perform a resource analysis.* Develop a resource plan that ensures that you have the resources necessary to gain access to the data you will need. I frequently consult with companies that don't take enough time to plan, and therefore don't realize what resources they will need in the future to effectively transfer data into the marketing data mart in order to support their email programs. How many people do you need to implement data transfers? Do you have the staff to perform an implementation? Does your organization have experience setting up automated data feeds between your internal (customer) databases and your external or internal service providers in order to support your dynamic marketing programs? What technical resources are associated with accessing the data from other parts of your organization?

4. *Perform an environment analysis.* Communicate your plans for the data to every department in your organization that might be impacted by the email marketing program and allow early feedback to ensure full organizational support. For example, would there be political resistance to moving data to an outsourced, externally hosted operating environment? When Wegmans Food Markets decided to outsource its email marketing program, management involved the internal technology team from the very beginning. The company had traditionally implemented and maintained all its own IT systems, so outsourcing was a major change that the information technology group needed to fully support. Because of its early involvement, IT became actively engaged in the design and strongly support the current programs.

IMPLEMENTING YOUR CONTACT PLAN

In Chapter 4 I discussed the importance of developing a strategic customer contact plan. Now it's time to implement it. Your contact plan can be as simple as sending an email to your entire customer base once a month or it can be a complicated mix of messages targeted at different segments and followed up with communication that takes into account recipients' responses to your previous messages. A successful plan must be well-defined and capable of being tracked and monitored over time. Customers, for example, may receive message B only if they have already received message A but did not click through on any links in the message. Or customers may receive one message every month until they make a purchase, at which point they will receive two follow-up messages: the first thanking them for the purchase, the second pointing to additional resources such as support and complementary products.

Regardless of the details of your company's specific plan, there are several steps that all organizations need to follow if their email marketing programs are going to be successful.

BUILDING A SCALABLE CUSTOMER PROFILE DATA MART

In 1997, Palm Inc. sent its very first marketing email to approximately 60,000 registered customers. While the effort was very successful—record numbers of customers visited the website, generating many sales and excellent feedback—Palm quickly realized that even this relatively small effort was placing undue strain on its internal resources. Although the email was fairly simple, containing no personalization and done in plain text, it took almost two months to set up and prepare the required servers and database. It also took two days to deliver the relatively low volume of emails, during which time Palm's internal network infrastructure experienced a severe overload. Once the emails had been delivered there was no data in the database allowing the marketers to quantify their success. They couldn't track customer response at the individual level and had no tools to allow them to access reports or analyze results. In short, the campaign had been a smashing success, but it did a better job of highlighting the possibilities of email-based customer communication than of allowing Palm to capitalize on these opportunities. What Palm realized it needed was a solution that would scale to meet its constantly growing demands and requirements.

When implementing the profile database such as the one Palm ended up using for its In Sync Online program, there's normally a one-time set up or data transfer followed by ongoing updates to the database. In some cases the ongoing updates will be made manually, such as when data needs to be imported to support a one-time email campaign. If data updates occur with any kind of regularity, develop scripts to automate those updates. Automating data updates is generally very efficient and makes the data much less susceptible to human errors. It's common to implement two-way data feeds that ensure that the profile database is synchronized with other databases containing shared information, such as purchase records and email response activity.

The only thing that's certain about your customer profiles is that they will change over time. For that reason, one of the most important design requirements for a customer profile database is that it be flexible and expandable. But designing for flexibility comes at a cost.

The greatest difficulty associated with modifying the structure of a customer database over time is the impact it has on data consistency. If, for example, a program has been operating for six months and a new field is added to the customer profile, this new field will naturally contain data only from the date it was added. Any reports run on data captured before the new field was added may contain gaps and inconsistent or confusing results.

When designing and implementing an email marketing data mart, you have two primary options: build and operate it yourself or outsource it.(I discuss different options for evaluating and selecting an email marketing platform in Chapter 9). Either way, the data mart will need to accommodate your program's anticipated growth. Three primary factors impact scalability and growth:

- *Data mart software and hardware platform.* You must choose your data mart platform based on its ability to support the transactional nature of your email marketing application. Your data mart hardware and software need to be able to function in a real-time environment where you're constantly interacting with the email marketing application, scheduling and delivering email, pulling reports, and designing and testing new campaigns.
- *Data size and complexity.* If you are keeping simple records on up to about 10,000 customers you can probably manage with a fairly simple data mart. If, on the other hand, you are building a complex customer model with millions of records, your system will have to be far more powerful.
- *Application and usage.* Will your organization send out one email newsletter every month, or will the data mart drive continuous customer communication? Are you taking batch data transfers once a week or getting real-time data updates throughout the day? Do you need to pull reports every few days, or are you constantly analyzing customer behavior and response activity?

Given the rapid growth that many online marketers and retailers are experiencing, it can be a challenge to plan for and stay ahead of growth. And although there are no standard formulas for determining the performance criteria for an email marketing data mart in order to have a safety margin, try to ensure that your data mart does not exceed 60 to 70 percent utilization at peak load. (Meaning that when the system is performing "flat out," it is only using 60 to 70 percent of the data mart's resources.) Once your system exceeds this threshold, it's time to begin upgrading or replacing hardware and software to increase your capacity.

EVALUATING APPLICATION TOOLS AND TECHNOLOGY

Although you can certainly build your own email marketing application, I strongly recommend buying one or working with a service provider. Keeping up with an industry of software application developers and email marketing service providers is too much trouble for most e-retailers and e-marketers. Whether you purchase software and have it installed on your own servers or work with an outside service provider who can host and operate your program will depend on factors which are discussed in Chapter 9. What's important are the capabilities of the technology platform, which will be the foundation of your email programs.

Judge the features of any technology platform relative to the marketing program you are implementing and how your organization plans to use it. In most cases you'll be better able to stay focused on your marketing program if you leave it to an outside service provider to manage the operations of the software platform. If you choose to bring an application in-house, though, you'll need to develop your own teams of technology, operations, and marketing experts to manage the programs' day-to-day operations. Here is a list of some of the technology platform requirements you may want to consider when choosing a service provider or implementing your own email marketing application

Ability to Customize the Program. How simple is it to customize the marketing application interface? Will your program be tailored to your needs and can you get customized reports on the results? Can you design your own customer applications, such as personal profile and sign-up pages, and can these pages contain any data elements you want? Can you give your email messages your own look and feel? Can you define the contact sequence? Can you designate any event as a trigger for communication? How well does the application support sophisticated data integration and synchronization between multiple databases? Will you end up with a truly customized marketing and customer communications program, or will you have an off-the-shelf mail delivery engine that you are responsible for operating? If for example, you want to segment your customers into teenagers, single twentysomethings, and baby boomer couples, do these segments show up in your marketing application so that you simply point and click to send the desired segment one of your email messages?

Access to Application User Interface. Does the technology platform have an application interface that enables you to plan, design, test, execute, and analyze your email marketing campaigns and programs? Is the interface a "thin client" (meaning that you don't have to download or install software on your computer)? Is it a Web-based application or an old-style client-server implementation that requires proprietary ("thick") client-side software to access the application? Does the marketing interface support multiple users with different levels of access privileges? For example, if you want to access the marketing application to run email campaigns or pull a program report from a number of different locations, can you do so simply using a Web browser? If not, you'll need to install custom client software on all computers that are going to access the system.

Level of Marketing Program Automation. How much of the marketing communication function can be automated? Can you automate the sequencing of your messages? Can data transfers be set up to be automatic, or do you have to follow application-specific manual procedures every time you want to import new data? Are participants in the message production process notified when certain stages in the process have been reached? Can message testing be automated? For example, there might be a built-in work-flow application that notifies everyone involved in the production and approval process whenever the program manager loads up the message content. Everyone can then inspect and comment on the message. When your legal department promotions group, quality assurance team, etc., have evaluated and approved the new email copy, is the program manager automatically notified with email receipts?

Ability to Define Sophisticated Business Rules. How easy is it to define complex custom business rules that enable events and profile data to be used to determine who receives messages? For example, "Send a message to everyone who received a promotion for a Louis Armstrong CD less than 60 days ago, clicked on the offer, but did not purchase the CD."

Event-Based Architecture. Are all customer interactions recorded as events? Is a history of events (i.e., message delivery, click through, purchase) kept in each customer's profile so that future communications can be targeted based on those events? Can the complete history of interactions with a customer or customer segment be used for reporting and analysis? For example, can you easily deliver a message to every person in your database who has been a member of your program for more than three months and clicked through from at least two emails? This would require that every contact event be stored in your data mart.

Level of Dynamic Message Personalization. Is each message dynamically and uniquely generated for each recipient? Can messages use any attribute in the customer profile to personalize the content? Can the "From" line and the "Subject" line an email message be personalized for each recipient? Can personalization rules be included in the message that generate new content based on profile data? For example, you should be able to generate a message saying something like: "You've told us your birthday is 6/22/62, making you 38 this June." This requires the personalization script to compute the age based on the birthday field in the profile.

Link Tracking by Individual. Does the technology platform reconfigure all Web links so that click throughs are automatically recorded in each email recipient's profile? For example, Handspring™ (www.handspring.com), a handheld computer company, sends a monthly newsletter to its customers. The newsletter includes links to its own products plus products from its developer community. It receives the links in standard form from the developers and pastes them straight into its email. Once the messages have been delivered, Handspring runs click-through reports tabulated by customer segment so that its developers can see how successful the campaign was. To accomplish this requires that every link is automatically reconfigured so it can be tracked at the individual level.

Ability to Define Individual Contact Limits. Can you define limits to the amount of email received at the individual customer level? Is it possible to give customers control of the number of emails they want to receive and automatically prioritize and deliver email in accordance with their personal limits and the overall limit set by your organization? For example, your company is running a sophisticated email marketing program with a variety of messages being delivered to a number of different customer segments. Weekly newsletters, promotions, and automatic messages such as tips and tricks, news alerts, birthday greetings, etc. are delivered to different customers every day. You've decided that no customer should receive more than two messages per week. To enforce this rule, you need to be able to set a systemwide limit that keeps track of all customer contacts and places a hold on delivery once the customer has reached his or her limit. Naturally, that hold should not apply to purchase confirmations, email responses from customer service, and the like. (See Chapter 10 for a discussion about coordinating and managing all of your customer communication through a single "communication gateway.")

Ability to Set Message Priorities. Can you prioritize messages so that the system knows which ones are most important if there are a limited number of contact opportunities in a given time period? Will the system automatically resume delivery of messages that were not delivered to certain individuals in the last time slot because those individuals had reached the contact limit and the messages were low priority? For example, a birthday greeting should always have highest priority. If you miss the opportunity to send someone a birthday greeting because other higher-priority messages were delivered before the birth date, there's hardly any sense sending them a greeting a week late.

Operational Reliability and Scalability. What reliability guarantees does the technology platform provider offer? Does the platform have a history of 24–7 operations? Can your platform or application provider demonstrate an ability to scale to meet current and future growth projections for your business? Can you get service-level agreements that guarantee the performance and operations of your program? For example, you have experienced phenomenal growth, going from 70,000 to 600,000 individuals in the email marketing data mart in under one year. Now you want to import data from your catalog database containing over 5 million customers, merge this information, and begin sending email to a subset of the catalog customers whose email addresses you captured. Is your system capable of handling this new load? Right now?

Ability to Use Sophisticated Data Models. Does the technology platform support sophisticated data analysis and data models? How do you access these data models? Can they be used to target and personalize your email messages? Can they be used for reporting and analysis? For example, you want to send a message to every customer your model indicated is in the Likely Deserter category. Each message is personalized with an offer that your model has predicted would be most relevant for that individual recipient.

Reporting and Analysis. Can reports be customized to match the specific needs of your organization? Are reports available at the individual level or only in aggregate form? How are the reports formatted? How are results displayed? Can the reports be integrated with current applications used by your marketing organization for reporting and analysis (such as Microsoft Excel) or are they stand-alone and reliant on specialized software applications? For example, you may want to generate a report of the number of customers who live in a given zip code area and who purchased something at least once every month over the last three months. And you might want to display the information cross-tabulated by the actual number of emails received.

Ability to Preview Message. Can you preview your messages before they're sent out? Can you set up test profiles so that you can adjust customer profile parameters and preview the effect this has on different elements of message personalization? Can you access and modify the personalization script and message content directly from within your application user interface?

Message Quality Assurance. How does the technology platform support the message production process to ensure that high-quality, perfectly spelled messages are delivered without broken Web links or personalization errors? Can any part of the quality assurance process be automated? How much control do you have over the test automation process? Can you send test messages to seed lists before running the full campaign to confirm that they'll be delivered correctly?

Ability to Develop Message Templates. Does the technology platform support "message templates" or "message masters" that can be reused for multiple campaigns? If you're delivering the same newsletter format with identical personalization elements every week, can a template be created to streamline the production process? For example, you send a weekly newsletter where the content is driven by each individual recipient's personal subscription profile. Your message template is set up once at the beginning of the program. Then each week you simply make a new copy of the template, insert the new content for that week's newsletter, and deliver the newsletter, which is already personalized, to each recipient based on the personalization scripts contained in the master template.

Support for One-time Data Import and Export. How easy is it to perform a one-time data import? Can data pulled into the system on a one-time basis be used for targeting, personalization, and reporting? How easy is it to do one-time data exports to external database? What formats are supported for one-time data imports and exports? Is there an application user interface that enables the marketer or system operator to easily select and import or export data? For example, you want to send a one-time email to all your customers who have contacted customer service in the last six months. To do so you'll need to import records into the email marketing data mart from your computer service database. The imported records would contain user ID and "issue codes" relating to why they contacted your support group. You import the customer service records, align them with the data in your email marketing data mart using the user ID, and send a personalized email to everyone who's had a recent support issue.

Message Turnaround Time and Scheduling. How long is the lag between Message Ready and Message Sent in the system? Can you set automatic delivery times for messages? For example, you are in the business of selling videos and DVDs. Once the Oscars have been awarded, you want to run an instant email program to your customer base offering a special Oscar package. The email needs to be scheduled for delivery as soon as the Oscars are complete and updated to highlight the new winners.

Automatic Detection of Appropriate Message Formats. Can the technology platform automatically determine the appropriate format (plain text, HTML, or AOL) for a message based on the recipients' email capabilities? Can customers have the option to override automatic message format detection and indicate their own preference? For example, when customers sign up for your email program, you automatically send them a welcome message. That message is set to detect whether the recipient's email program can read Web (HTML) mail or some other format, such as AOL. Depending on the result, the recipient's capabilities are noted in his or her profile and future emails are sent in the appropriate format.

Support for Autoreplies, Bounced Emails, and Live Responses. Does the technology platform automatically handle bounced email and automatic replies (i.e., "out-of-office" replies set up by email users to notify vendors that they are temporarily not reading their emails)? How are bounced emails processed? What determines that an email address is no longer active? Is a customer record containing a dead address kept in the data mart or discarded? How are nonstandard and personal replies handled? Is there support for automatic rerouting of incoming email? For example, the very first time you send a large number of emails to your customers, you might receive a high number of bounces. Over time you'll settle into a relatively predictable pattern, with only a fraction of a percentage of emails bouncing every month. But even when your email bounces, it's not necessarily because your customers are no longer reachable. The Internet is often temperamental and unpredictable. You must ensure that your technology platform can detect when an email address is truly dead and when you're just dealing with a server problem somewhere on the network.

Support for Live Profile Pages. Does the system support live, integrated profile pages that can be instantly accessed and modified by a customer? Can access to profile pages be protected with user name and password? Can the platform easily implement a password reminder service? For example, if a Palm InSync Online member forgets her InSync profile password, she can simply click the "Forgot my password" button. A new password is generated and the system instantly mails it to the email account on record. Within five minutes she's got a new password and has access to her profile, which she can inspect, update, or modify.

Support for Unsubscribe. What types of unsubscribe requests does the technology platform support? Does it support standard "reply unsubscribe" procedures where the recipient replies to an email and types "Unsubscribe" in the subject header? Do the outbound emails integrate easily with live profile pages where recipients can modify or update their personal subscriptions with a single click? In every email you'll want to include a link that encourages recipients to update their current profiles so that they receive exactly what they want instead of unsubscribing in frustration.

Customer Service Integration. Are customer profiles easily accessible to the customer service organization? Can customer service manually unsubscribe customers or update their personal profile information through this interface? For example, if your 1-800-support operators need to access email profiles, they should be able to do so directly through a Web interface. If a customer calls your support center asking to be removed from your email program and the change doesn't take effect for a while due to infrequent data updates among different systems, you stand the chance of upsetting him by delivering additional marketing emails before the profile is updated.

IMPLEMENTING CUSTOMER PROFILE PAGES

Customer profile pages are the part of your website where customers can sign up, subscribe, examine, and update the personal information that you maintain in your profile database. Consider the following when implementing customer profile pages:

Make the Profile Page Live. Connect the profile page directly to the profile database so that any information entered or accessed from the page will be written and read directly to the profile database in real time. There are several advantages to live profile pages. Subscribers like interacting with a system that always displays the most current information. They get a sense of being in control when their information is easily accessible. Live profile pages also let you customize what visitors see based on information they are currently submitting or on what you already know about them. For instance, if a user indicates the sports he likes on the first page of a subscription, the next page will ask only questions pertaining to those sports. Live profile pages should be integrated with all email communication that is generated from the profile, and every email should contain a link inviting the customer to come back and update or modify his or her profile.

Hosting the Profile Page. This means running the application that displays the profile page, giving the subscriber access to it, and connecting it with the underlying profile database. Profile pages can be run off either a central customer database containing all customer information or the email marketing data mart. If a new profile is created when a subscriber signs up or an existing subscriber modifies a profile, the changes to that profile are written to whichever database it is connected to. This database then needs to update other databases that contain duplicates of the profile information. The lag time between when a profile gets modified and when the information is updated in other databases may impact the performance and responsiveness of your email programs. If, for instance, the profile pages are not connected in real time to the email database, a subscriber who has just updated a profile may receive an email reflecting the old profile. Or, as we mentioned above, she may continue to receive email even after unsubscribing, which can generate needless customer service complaints.

Profile-Page Security and Access Controls. If a profile page contains personal information about the subscriber, access to that page must be restricted. Customer name and password are the highest degree of security. Some companies use "cookies" that save a subscriber's name and password on the subscriber's computer. This enables the subscriber to access her profile from that specific computer without having to enter a user name or password. One potential problem with this approach is that it makes it easy for anyone with access to the subscriber's computer to view—and potentially change—the profile. However, it's still difficult for someone using a different computer to access the profile and compromise security. Because subscribers sometimes forget the specific user names and passwords they signed up with, it's important to provide password reminder services. You might also want to provide an automatic mail-back service that sends an email containing the new password to the subscriber's email address on record.

For lower-level security concerns, asking subscribers to enter their email addresses may be enough. Another way to protect a profile is to give access through a weblink that is automatically emailed to the profile owner's email address. This is essentially what EGreetings.com or Blue Mountain do when they send you an email notifying you that someone has sent you an electronic greeting card. The email contains a link with a private ID that takes you right to the private web page containing your card. To modify a profile using this scheme, the subscriber must go to the profile web page and enter his or her email address or other security information. If there is a profile in the system for that email address, a link with an embedded time-limited password is sent out. When recipients click on the link, they're taken straight to their profile page.

Distributed versus Integrated Profiles. If you offer a wide range of information, products, or services, you need to choose between implementing distributed or integrated profiles. Distributed profiles generally reside in multiple databases and can include separate profiles for each product, service, group, etc. For example, a large company like Hewlett Packard, which has a wide range of products, may implement separate profiles for its different divisions. Integrated or unified profiles are centralized solutions where all subscriptions can be accessed through a single profile. For instance, when you sign up with more than one of the Yahoo! services such as MyYahoo!, free email, calendar, etc., Yahoo! will recognize you and let you sign up for the new service using the information you've already provided when you previously signed up. Centralizing the customer profile allows you to view all customer interactions from one place and gives customers a sense that you know them, regardless of the product or division they are interacting with. Customer-centered organizations should always opt for the integrated profile.

IMPLEMENTING A MESSAGE-PRODUCTION PROCESS

Implementing a message production process is one way to ensure that the inevitable complications associated with generating high-quality, timely email communication don't overwhelm your organization. A message production process may consist of a checklist containing every step of the process. Using the checklist ensures that you won't stray from the defined processes you have put in place to develop and deliver messages. Each part of the process should be signed off by the appropriate team before moving on to the next part. Use the following steps as a guideline for implementing a production process.

Describe the Production Cycle. The production cycle takes you from message conception to final delivery. Questions that must be answered in order to describe the production cycle may include: How often does each type of message get delivered (monthly, weekly, daily)? What steps are involved in getting a new campaign launched (approvals, resource allocation, content development, data access, and use)? What are the relationships between teams involved in producing the message?

Identify All Contributors in the Production Process. Normally, several interdepartmental dependencies are involved in producing a message or running a program. As we discussed earlier, the relationship marketing manager and his or her team owns the production process. Yet their success depends on having identified all participating contributors.

Depending on the nature of your business, consider involving some or all of the following parts of your organization during program activation or campaign execution:

- *Production.* It goes without saying that the production team (including graphic designers, copy writers, etc.) should be notified well in advance of a campaign.
- *Legal.* Check your program or campaign for legal compliance with your privacy statement, applicable state laws, federal laws and, if appropriate, international laws.
- *Customer service.* Ensure that customer service is informed of and familiar with any programs or campaigns that may result in inbound traffic.
- *Sales.* Make sure that your sales department is aware of any direct communication with customers.
- *Merchandising.* Check products included in email for correct photo, pricing, copy, availability, etc.
- *Fulfillment.* Confirm availability and ability to deliver within implied time frames.
- *IT or web services.* Ensure that necessary information technol-

ogy support is available and that there are no conflicts, such as scheduled website maintenance.

- *Quality assurance.* Make sure that your quality assurance team is aware of each new program or campaign and any unique requirements associated with it.
- *Outside service providers.* Notify any and all affected service providers.

Identify Review Points in the Production Process. These may include initial message design review, a targeting and personalization review, a legal review, and a quality review. The final review in the production process will normally be one or more test mailings (using "seed lists") designed to evaluate the actual communication and make sure that all personalization and targeting elements of the message are working. You may want to consider creating two seed lists for test mailings. The first is your production seed list, the second is an approval seed list.

Identify Repeating and Predictable Events. Emailing your "New Releases" campaign to your customers will run more smoothly and efficiently if you implement a predictable schedule, such as every Thursday morning, instead of an irregular one.

Identify Production Dependencies. All data that will drive a program must be available in the database before testing can begin. And obviously copy needs to be written before your legal department can approve it. Understanding and mapping out the dependencies in your production process is critical to streamlining the process and maximizing resource utilization.

Identify Production Cycle Risks. Because a single snag in your production process can easily delay the entire program, you must identify your program's weakest links. If there are any high-risk parts of the production process, call them out and evaluate how their failure will impact the overall success of your program. Develop a process for communicating production-related problems to all interested parties so you can minimize the impact of any unexpected delays.

MESSAGE PRODUCTION

For purposes of this discussion, we're assuming that you already know what your message will be about—a corporate newsletter, a special offer, a post-purchase follow-up, an automatic reminder, or anything else. We're also assuming that you have a production process in place and that you're ready to produce the actual content of your messages. Here are some things you will need to plan for.

CREATIVE, INTERACTIVE DESIGN

Capturing the attention of the recipient is the most significant challenge facing your program. The message design should engage recipients, causing them to consider your messages, think about what you are communicating, and respond appropriately.

A good creative designer can give even a plain-text email some personality and attitude and make it look fun and appealing. Messages should be designed to support three formats: plain text, HTML, and AOL. HTML allows designers to include forms, buttons, and other Web controls. Text and graphics for an email message must be designed to achieve maximum impact while staying within the parameters of the contact plan and maintaining the customer's overall brand experience.

Creative design for email messages is different than for other media. Incorporating links, active media such as Macromedia Flash, streaming audio, and even video clips, email looks more and more like the Web and allows for a fair amount of interactivity. For example, Wildbrain Inc., a leading animation studio, engages its viewers by using the voices of the stars of its animations in its "webisode alert" emails. The email graphics announcing new episodes look like oversized movie tickets with animated characters right on the stub. A single click on the ticket takes the viewer straight to the wildbrain.com website and launches the new webisode. wildbrain.com's mailings routinely generate a 45 to 60 percent response rate.

But email is also very different from the Web. First of all, on the Web, users are in self-service mode; they're there because they want to be. With email, on the other hand, *you* initiated the communication. This means that not everyone will be happy about downloading large audio or image-heavy files. So when considering your email message's creative design, consider the bandwidth constraints that the recipient may be operating under. For instance, consider having the first paragraph of an article with a link pointing to the remainder on your website, as opposed to including the whole article in the email.

Effective email should have a communications and service feel. The recipient should be able to determine at a glance whether the email is appropriate; if it isn't, it will be discarded quickly. You may be tempted to fill your emails with detailed laundry lists describing every offer, every special, and every new piece of information you have. This type of communication is not particularly effective because it's not targeted: it's only relevant if the recipient inadvertently stumbles across something interesting. In those rare instances when you truly must include a large amount of information in an email, at least create a "table of contents" with links that automatically scroll to the appropriate places in the document.

Have a design specialist focused on email create your email messages. Depending on how many you're doing and how much new design input you need each time, it may make sense to bring your message design function in-house. If not, you can always hire outside consultants.

WRITING MESSAGE COPY

How do you write to encourage engagement? Good, effective email copy has a distinct voice and feel. It's usually short and action-oriented. And depending on the brand relationship you're trying to build, it may also be authoritative, formal, friendly, jovial, or casual. Like the design, your email copy must support the customer's experience of your brand. When eBags communicates with its customers through the My eBags program, every email is signed by Jon Nordmark, eBags' cofounder and CEO. eBags decided to engage its customers by writing its emails with Jon's personal tone and voice to reinforce the fact that all accompanying special offers, product recommendations, and other lifestyle-driven content is endorsed by

Jon himself. This strategy also supports the friendly, trustworthy nature of the brand, and how important each individual member is to eBags. And it seems to be working. Now, when customers call, send email, or engage in live one-on-one chat sessions with eBags customer service professionals, they often refer to the email they received from Jon. They will even sometimes send correspondence to Jon directly.

But be careful: Sending emails from your CEO doesn't always work, particularly if the CEO has poor name recognition. One retailer used an in-house software program to send out plain-text and HTML messages from its CEO. But the HTML went out as an *attachment* to the plain-text email. And the CEO was not well-known by name. As a result, recipients took one look at the email, saw it was from someone they didn't know, saw that it had an attachment, and figured it was either spam or a virus. The open rates for the company's newsletter averaged an abysmal 3 percent. Working with a service provider to fix the program the company was able to increase its open rate to a staggering 40 percent. It now uses an automatic detection feature to determine what format email each recipient can receive and sends the email in the appropriate platform. The from line now reads "The *Company*Scene" and sends out an automatic "Welcome and thank you for signing up" message, reinforcing and reiterating the value subscribers can expect to receive within 12 hours of signing up.

Bottom line? Whether you have in-house or third-party copy writers, make sure they have plenty of experience writing email copy.

PERSONALIZING THE MESSAGE

A personalization script is essentially a small computer program that looks at the data record or profile for each recipient and generates the actual, personalized email. The simplest personalization scripts insert the recipient's first name as a greeting at the beginning of the email. More complex personalization scripts look at several elements of a profile and generate dynamic content, uniquely tailored to each recipient. This might be anything from calculating and including the address of the nearest retail store to making reference to the recipient's age or birth date. When Petopia sends its email newsletters to customers who have registered for the *Petopia Post*, the newsletters are personalized to include content relating to the type of pet customers have. Dog owners get the dog column; cat owners get the cat column. People who own both get both.

There is no single personalization scripting language. Some applications have developed proprietary scripting languages, while others use more standard languages such as JavaScript. Personalization is performed by either a technically trained Web developer or a software programmer who is familiar with the system. Poorly written personalization scripts can result in customers receiving erroneous or inaccurate messages. Therefore, always be sure to thoroughly test any kind of personalization before sending out your mailing. (See the discussion on "quality assurance" later in this section.)

TARGETING THE MESSAGES

The criteria for targeting your messages will be outlined in your contact plan. Generally speaking, though, there are several ways of targeting. If you're using lists to send out messages, you'll do your targeting when the list is extracted, selecting only those names that meet the targeting criteria. Then hand the list over to the mailer application or service bureau you're using and have them deliver the messages. If you're using a database-driven, continuous-relationship marketing system to drive customer communication, you'll select your targeting criteria before the messages are generated. The system will then automatically send a message to the people who match the criteria. The person responsible for a campaign or program normally selects each message's targeting criteria, which means that he or she must be familiar with the customer data profile, the contact strategy, and the contact plan.

TIMING THE MESSAGES

Timing is key to much of the success of direct marketing. For regularly scheduled messages, the timing criteria will simply map to the contact plan. These criteria may be simple; for example, a market analysis newsletter that is delivered every Friday afternoon after the close of the stock markets. And you may be able to automate much of the process of responding to predictable events such as holidays, anniversaries, or birthdays. But if message delivery is tied to unpredictable or irregular events such as weather conditions or customer purchases, you have to use more complex timing criteria to trigger communication. Your ability to automate event-driven actions will depend on your message production process and technology platform or service provider. An online retailer may want to automatically sample every tenth customer one week after they make a purchase. The retailer could design a program to automatically send an email (in the form of a simple Web survey) asking for input. eBags reaps phenomenal success from a program like this. The company solicits product ratings and testimonials from customers 30 days after they make a purchase. Over 30 percent of customers respond to this offer, which, by the way, is accompanied by an incentive. This program not only strengthens eBags' relationship with its existing customers; each product's aggregate rating also serves as valuable site content for prospects and other repeat customers who want to be sure that they are buying the perfect bag or accessory for themselves or someone they know. All product testimonials appear on the eBags site for users to read.

The person who is responsible for your campaign or program is normally the one who selects the message timing criteria. When message delivery is automated, you need to continuously monitor your messages to ensure that they're performing properly.

QUALITY ASSURANCE

Unfortunately, mistakes in the message production process are far from uncommon, especially given the constant time pressures, the enormous potential for personalization-related errors, and the range of email programs people use. There are several different ways to ensure that messages delivered meet your quality criteria. Depending on your technology platform, you may be able to automate the process of checking for broken links and verifying personalization scripts. As was discussed earlier you may also be able to perform a quality assurance check by sending a test message to a seed list. Any errors that come up in this process can be corrected before sending the mailing to the entire list.

You must evaluate the quality of your program on a regular and ongoing basis. This can be done in two ways: (1) evaluate the response that the program is generating relative to the goals outlined in your contact plan; (2) monitor direct customer feedback. Declining response rates, climbing unsubscribe requests, or an increase in customer service complaints may all be indicators of developing quality problems.

Any message production team needs to include a dedicated quality control function. Normally this responsibility is handled by a person or team that understands the contact plan behind a message as well as the technical workings of the email technology platform.

DEVELOPING MESSAGE TEMPLATES

Think of a message template as a reusable or generic message that contains all standard elements of a message, such as graphics, layout, personalization elements, and so on. Your entire production team is normally involved in developing message templates, which are an effective way to both streamline your production process and increase the consistency and quality of the messages you deliver. If you're going to send a particular message out only once, there's obviously no need for a template. But if you're going to produce it on a regular basis, a template can really help. A well-designed message template should contain copy guidelines and reusable content elements, such as a graphic header for a newsletter, reusable personalization scripts, and a test script. It may also contain targeting selections and timing rules. When these elements of a template are in place, all that's left is to drop in the actual text and graphics for each new message. CDNOW produces a large number of personalized emails that range from daily industry news to weekly new releases and frequent special promotions. Each type of email has its own template, enabling CDNOW to produce its messages very effectively and efficiently.

Keep in mind that different technology platforms and email

marketing service providers may support message templates differently. It is therefore important to consider how a given system's template will address your program needs.

OPERATING THE PROGRAM

You're now ready to flip the switch and activate your customer communications program. Once it's active, your subscribers will begin to rely on and anticipate your communication. As we discussed earlier, 90 percent of the response activity to your email communication will come in within the first 48 hours after your email is delivered. Monitoring and tracking this response activity is an integral part of any program. The technology platform used to operate the program must therefore be fully operational on a 24-7 basis, not just during the time when messages are being delivered. Consider for instance one of the "digital VCR" products that lets you digitally record television programs onto a built-in hard drive. When the manufacturer sends emails to its customers, you could imagine them including the week's television schedule in the email, perhaps even enabling you to select which programs you want your "digital VCR" to record from within the email and then have it program your device to automatically record your favorite shows. In a scenario such as this, customers may access their email with the weekly television schedule any time of day or night during the week. In other words, the email must be live and enable customers to interact with it whenever they want, 24 hours per day.

Imagine the email service run by brokerage firms such as E*TRADE® that sends you a copy of your complete investment portfolio at the end of the trading week. A lot of E*TRADE®'s customers would have heart attacks if their email suddenly didn't show up one Friday. The operational reliability of email marketing programs is a very important part of ensuring customer satisfaction.

Operating a continuous email marketing program requires a dedicated operations staff. As was discussed earlier in this chapter, the operations staff consists of both technical, systems-level operations people and marketing personnel. The technical personnel are responsible for 24-7 operations, while marketing is responsible for overseeing and managing message production and for continuously tracking the quality of and response to your programs.

RUNNING TESTS

The effectiveness of a program can only be determined through on-going testing. This means that when you first implement and operate your email marketing service, a good portion of your efforts will be focused on running tests. As we discussed earlier, your contact plan should include a message test plan that defines your test criteria and specifies the type of testing each message requires. When you're testing you'll naturally follow the test plan, but you'll also constantly be updating and modifying it. Testing is only effective if it is dynamic, leaving room for flexibility and change. (Also see Chapter 8 for more information on measuring and tracking your email marketing programs.)

RUNNING REPORTS

There are two different approaches to reporting. One is to generate all reports from the email marketing data mart in real time. The other is to run batch reports, downloading and displaying selected data sets at the desktop level. Each has advantages and disadvantages. Pulling reports live from the data mart provides access to the entire data set for every report and offers the most flexibility. The downside is that every time a report needs to be displayed or a different view taken on the data, a "round-trip" request needs to be made to the data mart. This means that the entire data set has to be accessed to display any changes or updates in a report, a process that can be slow and increase performance overhead on the data mart, which is also being used by other applications such as email delivery.

To perform batch reports, you have to select a broad set of reporting criteria and generate a data subset from the data mart. This data subset is then downloaded to the marketer's and analyst's computer desktops, where it can be displayed and manipulated without communicating with the reporting server. The disadvantage here is that any data that's not in the reporting subset can't be accessed without generating a new subset. In addition, generating a complex data subset and downloading it from the data mart to the desktop can be a time-consuming process. Still, the advantages of this approach tend to outweigh the disadvantages, because once the data is on the desktop it is instantly available and no further communication with the data mart is required. The data set can be manipulated instantaneously. Overall, responsiveness with the batch approach is much higher once the appropriate data set has been selected. If you are going to be performing complex analysis of your data, you will probably want to separate it from the (transactional) database used to personalize, deliver, and track email.

CUSTOMIZING REPORTS

Customizing reports means providing access to custom data elements in order to analyze and tabulate them so that you can monitor your program's performance and evaluate each of your tests, campaigns, and ongoing programs. Since the data driving an email marketing program will be customized on a program-by-program basis, it naturally follows that reports need to be customized the same way. A natural health products retailer has developed customized reports that enable it to look at purchase behavior by individual consumers down to the product level. The company can measure the effectiveness of its email program on a short-term and long-term basis by keeping a complete history of all purchases and all email response activity and correlating the two through customized reports.

Customized reports sometimes require data that isn't available for the specific email marketing program they are supporting. For instance, if transactional information—such as the revenue generated from a promotional campaign—isn't a part of the data mart, it must be integrated separately into reports so that individual campaigns can be correlated with the results they generate. Customizing reports may therefore involve setting up additional data feeds. In general, though, if the data is available for reports, it should be integrated into the entire program and also made available for modeling, targeting, scheduling, and personalizing the marketing programs. Setting up separate data feeds exclusively for the purpose of supporting customized reports should always be considered a short-term solution.

Sometimes it makes more sense to export the data generated by an email marketing program in order to make it available from within other reporting applications. When Wegmans implemented its email marketing program it decided to use this approach. Wegmans gains an understanding of how to better anticipate and service its customers' needs by performing analyses on the market basket data that it gathers from customers as they make their purchases with their Wegmans Shopper Club Card. It was much easier to incorporate its email data into its existing analysis and reporting infrastructure than to export all the other data into the email marketing data mart.

A number of display vehicles are used for analyzing, displaying, and manipulating data and results. The most common of these is Microsoft Excel, which you may already be comfortable using. Customizing Excel spreadsheets by incorporating different data sets and integrating information from an email marketing report is a relatively simple operation—even for a non-techie. There are also a number of proprietary, application-specific reporting front-ends and a series of customizable reporting tool sets that offer sophisticated displays and data manipulation capabilities. Some of these applications are very powerful, but often they're simply overkill.

Whatever your destination, the only way to get there is one step at a time. There aren't any shortcuts on the road to creating a successful email marketing program. In this chapter we covered a lot of ground. We saw how important it is to make it easy for your customers to sign up and to unsubscribe. We discussed developing and implementing procedures for handling complaints. We covered program staffing and the importance of understanding data, where it resides, and how to access it. Finally, we discussed all the steps that lead to actual program implementation, from creating a marketing data mart and writing copy to developing a message production process and testing. But after all this, how can you tell whether your program is really working? In Chapter 8 we'll find out, as we cover the specifics of analyzing data and defining and measuring success.

MEASURING AND TRACKING SUCCESS

Y OU CAN ALWAYS recognize direct marketers: they're the ones who never feel they've tested and analyzed their marketing programs enough. They're constantly measuring their efforts and tracking their results. But what are they really looking for? In this chapter we'll take a look at how to use quantitative and qualitative methods to develop success criteria: in other words, how to test, measure, track, and analyze how effective and successful your Internet direct marketing campaigns and programs are.

UNDERSTANDING WHAT SUCCESS IS

One of the most difficult challenges of Internet direct marketing is to clearly articulate what success is and how you're going to measure it. How can you define success, for example, when each one of your customers is receiving a different email message with different content and offers? Do traditional direct marketing measurement techniques apply online? One thing is certain, you won't be able to figure out whether you're meeting your goals if you don't develop measurable success criteria.

Companies use a number of different measures to define success. They range from the traditional revenue per email, to response rates (measured by click-through) to improved brand awareness and customer satisfaction as measured by surveys and customer service activity. Whether you choose one of these or some other measure, the first step is to define how you're going to track your performance over time.

Newly launched email marketing programs, for example, often enjoy 30 to 40 percent response rates to the first emails sent to an existing customer base. But it usually doesn't take long for those numbers to slip well under 10 percent, which is the industry average for fairly untargeted communication. Dropping from 30 percent to below 10 percent doesn't mean that the program is a failure; it may only mean that the initial results were high due to pent-up expectations and the novelty of a new program. Once customers see what the program has to offer, they settle into more predictable response patterns. That said, no Internet direct marketer should be happy with single-digit response rates. Following the guidelines and principles outlined in this book, it is possible to design programs with sustainable response rates well above 10 percent.

As you define the success criteria of a particular Internet direct marketing program, you first have to understand both the customer behaviors that such a program may elicit and the metrics that can be used to gauge these behaviors. Table 8-1 provides a framework to organize these behaviors and metrics and lays out schematically an online customer's relationship with a company from acquisition to retention.

One online retailer who ran a sweepstakes promotion to capture new leads got very excited by click-through rates of over 15 percent on follow-up email. Upon further analysis, though, the company discovered that the people who clicked through generally had no intention of engaging further; response to later communications was very low, and conversion rates barely noticeable. The high initial response came because people had signed up to win a prize and were responding to see whether there was more information about the contest. When the retailer did a post-campaign analysis, it concluded that each new customer acquired through the sweepstakes had cost them about $700. Hardly a successful program by any standard.

Clearly, measuring only click-throughs and online conversion to purchase rates is not always enough to determine the success of a

Table 8-1 Customer Engagement Continuum

Marketer's Objective	Customer Attitude or Goal	Customer Behavior	Metric
Acquisition	I am interested in your company.	Visits website	Number of site visits; length of stay
	I want a specific product or service.	Purchases from website	Sales; acquisition cost per customer
	I want to receive email.	Opts-in to content stream	Number of subscribers; acquisition cost per subscriber
Retention and Loyalty	I am reading what you are sending me.	Opens email	Open rate per message delivered
	I am interested in the information you provide.	Clicks on links in email	Click-through rate per message delivered
	The offers you extend are relevant to me.	Purchases products	Revenue per promotional message delivered
	Your program continues to hold my interest.	Maintains subscription; visits website without prompting; modifies profile; participates in surveys	Rate of subscriber base that has unsubscribed; number of site visits; survey results
	I am loyal to your company.	Purchases more products; makes unprompted purchases; refers friends	Lifetime value per customer

given email marketing campaign. This is especially true if you're doing business in multiple channels, such as Web, catalog (telephone), and retail. Victoria's Secret has been very successful in correlating catalog telephone sales with their emails by tracking all purchases made on the Web and through the catalog for the ten days immediately following delivery of an email mailing. What it found was that an astonishingly high percentage of customers who receive an email and buy within ten days make their purchase by phone. Had the company not tracked sales across both their online store and call centers, it would not have included a significant portion of sales and the success of its email marketing program would have been much less evident.

TRACKING SUCCESS THROUGH CONTINUOUS TESTING

Testing is an integral part of all direct marketing—whether online or off—because it shows us what our customers like and don't like. But testing serves a very different purpose offline and online largely because the cost of offline contact is very high, especially when one considers that incremental cost online is essentially zero. Offline, tests of single campaigns are generally made to determine the cost-effectiveness of the campaign. Online, however, tests can be designed to measure the impact of email marketing programs on long-term customer relationships as well as the total long-term ROI of the program.

What we most want to monitor and control is the *annoyance factor:* the cost of overcontacting customers. When customers feel as though they are receiving too many irrelevant messages they stop paying attention or disengage completely. Thus, the most significant fallout from sending too much (or untargeted) unpersonalized email is that you lose the opportunity for future contact. One online retailer started losing its most profitable customers when its emails began focusing more and more on pure promotional contact. Every email included some kind of "$10 off," or "buy two, get one free" offer. As a result, less price-sensitive customers started getting annoyed because nobody seemed to be paying attention to the reason they had signed up for the program in the first place: to receive relevant, informational emails that would help them select products. At the same time, though, the program generated lots of new revenue from the retailers' less profitable segments: those who had signed up because of the great prices and specials. In the long run, the shift to more promotional email ended up having a very negative impact on the company's ability to reach profitability. Testing in email marketing, then, is focused on optimizing the contact sequence to facilitate long-term engagement and maximize the value of each and every customer.

That said, it's still very important to test your individual promotional campaigns as well. Knowing that the annoyance factor is low and that your customers find your contact amusing and informative is going to be helpful only if your email marketing program is meeting its goals. Promotions that result in below-average response and conversion and that don't generate any revenue probably aren't going to be sustainable even if customers are thrilled by the entertainment value or informational content of what they're receiving. While Victoria's Secret has a (limited) male segment that enjoys receiving emails for their sexy content alone, the marketers behind these email programs are very aware of how every campaign performs from a financial standpoint. Sure, they look at click-through activity as a leading indicator of interest, but they always take it a step further by tracking the conversion rate of every campaign. This helps them carefully monitor the cost-effectiveness of their emails.

While testing an offline direct marketing program usually takes weeks or months, testing with email is normally done in a matter of days, sometimes less. One of the advantages of the quick turnaround and lower cost of online testing is that you can test continuously and make it a normal part of the fabric of any customer communications and marketing program. For instance, when Illuminations sends out an email campaign, it usually also mails out printed catalogs to a control group. It then measures the conversion rates between those in the control group and those who received the emails. Across the board, emails perform better than the catalog—in some instances by 20 percent, in others by as much as 100 percent. And that's only looking at conversion rates; it doesn't take into consideration the much higher cost of contact for the postal mailings. Interestingly enough, Illuminations had its best results ever from a mailing that sent a postcard and an email to the same customers. Conversion to purchase was almost 11 percent.

One of the most interesting challenges you face when designing tests for your email marketing programs is how to deal with the highly individualized messages you're sending. In traditional direct marketing, you'd hold as many variables as possible constant, vary one, and measure the differences in response. You might, for instance, deliver the same mail promotion to a sample of customers but send different creative designs to different subgroups. Or you could keep the creative designs constant while testing different promotional offers to see which one performs best. This type of testing works fine for basic email campaigns where large groups of people get the same message. But what happens when the messages that customers receive are automatically triggered by their behavior and when no two people receive exactly the same contact (or content) in the same order?

In these cases, instead of testing for single variables, you need to design your tests to measure criteria that span a number of relevant parts of the customer relationship. These may include factors such as click-through rates, cumulative purchases, unsubscribe rates, and even a customer satisfaction index. What we're most interested in is the *response curve*, that is, response activity over time. Table 8-2 outlines some additional elements you may be able to test for.

So how much testing is enough? When does testing result in diminishing returns and when are we leaving money on the table? Should you always test a new campaign or program before launching it? If your program is going to run on a continuous basis, you should test different variants of the communication on a regular schedule to ensure that you are maximizing the returns from the program and keeping it fresh. I have seldom if ever come across a program that's been tested too much. Every time you run a well-designed test, you'll learn something that you can use to make your future programs better.

REPORTING AND ANALYSIS

Too many people make the mistake of lumping reporting and analysis together, but although they are closely related, they're very different. Reports describe *what happened* and help us understand a past situation (such as a campaign). Analysis looks

Table 8-2 Test Criteria in Email Marketing

Contact frequency	Vary contact frequency by segment and within segments to determine optimal contact frequencies.
Contact sequencing	The order and timing of customer contacts can have a big impact on the results of an email contact plan. You can also control how contact is sequenced in response to various events and triggers.
Self-reported vs. observed information	Compare the effectiveness of contact that strictly adheres to self-reported interests with contact based on observed and implied interests. If you are using observed information that could be in conflict with self-reported information, monitor customer complaints and feedback to ensure that you are not annoying your customers.
Promotional vs. informational contact mix	Testing determines which customers prefer to receive purely promotional contact and which find this too pushy and would prefer a softer, more informal approach. The optimal mix is determined by varying the content within messages (e.g., 70 percent editorial, 30 percent promotional) as well as the overall contact mix (e.g., two informational messages for every one promotional).
Personalization and individualized contact	Testing can help determine whether the added complexity of individualized contact or even just personalized messages can justify the extra effort (and cost).

for *current insight and meaning*; it's where we gain new understanding that we can act on going forward. What distinguishes the email programs of an experienced direct marketer such as Victoria's Secret from most others is its constant analysis. The company is always looking for answers in the data and always trying to improve the effectiveness of its programs through the findings that its analysis uncovers.

Reporting is perhaps the most commonly used feature of any email marketing solution. You must closely integrate it with the day-to-day operations of your campaigns and programs to ensure you get the best information and feedback. Reports enable you to track and measure the performance of campaigns and ongoing programs, validating their viability and detecting possible problems.

While reporting is a tactical, everyday portion of email marketing, analysis is strategic. It looks at the history of the interactions you've had with your customers and uses this history to better understand what they like and dislike, who they are, who responds to what, which ones are most valuable, and so forth. When developing new email marketing programs, it's common to analyze and model existing data and to evaluate results from past email campaigns. This analysis will reveal behavior and response patterns, help determine natural customer segmentations, and clarify the tests that will give you the greatest insight into your customers' behavior.

Performing analysis is a two-phase process. The *design phase* lays out the information you're looking for: the insights and results you're trying to uncover and the tools and techniques you'll use. The *technical phase* uses the design from phase one to perform the actual data analysis.

Your analysis will generally have one or two basic outcomes. The first is to develop new reports that give you direct access to the information discovered during analysis. The second is to develop new segmentations that enable more precise targeting and personalization. If, for instance, you discover that a number of your customers buy only on weekends, you might develop a new segmentation called "Weekend Buyers." Having done this, you can target and personalize messages for the weekend buyer with specific content, and you can generate reports that illustrate how they respond to the communications they are receiving.

Let's take a look at a few different analysis and modeling techniques.

DETERMINING YOUR CUSTOMERS' PRESENT AND FUTURE VALUE

In traditional direct mail and database marketing it's common to measure and predict the value of individual customers based on their past history and actions. Recency, frequency, and monetary (RFM) and life-time value (LTV) analysis measures, predicts, and tracks long-term customer value.

RFM analysis can be effectively applied to promotion-oriented email marketing programs, but sometimes it is limited because of the much richer data sets we're operating with online. A study done by Boston Consulting Group, entitled "State of Online Retailing 2.0," found that pure-play online retailers generated an average of 10 percent of their revenue from nonretail activities such as advertising and affiliate referrals. For that reason, I propose a technique that I call recency, frequency, and click-value (RFC) analysis. "Click-value" is a measure of the value generated from a customer who is exposed to (opens) or responds to (clicks through) a particular email. Depending on the application, value is generated if the link results in a purchase or advertising exposure, generates referral fees, or drives site traffic. The average click-value for an email marketing program or campaign is determined by calculating the total value generated by the email divided by the total number of advertising exposures (assuming that the email contains revenue-generating advertisements) and responses (click-throughs). Remember, though, not all links generate the same click-value.

Your Internet direct marketing effort cannot reach its potential unless you predict the future value of your customers. Doing so will help you track how much you can safely invest in building a dialogue with prospects and customers while ensuring overall program success (and profitability) at the same time. The most common method for measuring future value is to perform life-time value (LTV) calculations. LTV—just like RFM—applies only to a limited subset of email marketing applications. That's why we prefer to use life-time click-value (LTCV) as a measure. You can also use a customer satisfaction index (CSI) to track future value because any significant downward movement can be a strong indicator of poor future performance.

Table 8-3 summarizes some common applications of these forms of analysis.

Table 8-3 Customer Value Analysis Methods and Their Applications

Analysis Method	How It Works	Associated Applications
RFM analysis	Calculates a score for each customer based on a combination of last purchase, purchase frequency, and total (or average) amount spent	To identify most valuable customers To predict propensity to respond at different price points and with different incentives To identify likely defectors To identify optimal timing and sequencing To identify cross-sell and up-sell opportunities
RFC	Scores each customer based on a combination of last email click-through, click-through frequency, and total click-value	Same applications as RFM plus: To measure success of non-promotional contact To measure customer value based on factors such as "community value," not just purchase activity To identify which customers are most engaged (not exclusively as a measure of purchase activity) To measure effectiveness of response
LTV	Predicts the net profit of a customer over an extended time based on past purchase	To predict a life-time value of a new customer To determine the

Analysis method	How It Works	Associated Applications
	history or assumptions about future purchase activity, retention rates and total program costs, and performing net present value (NPV) calculations.	probability of success of a new program To measure the impact of new customer acquisition vs. retention-based marketing investments
LTCV	Predicts the net "click-profit" of a customer over an extended time, based on past click activity or assumptions about future click activity, retention rates and total program costs, and performing net present value (NPV) calculations	Same applications as LTV plus: To determine expected future value for nonpurchase behavior
CSI	Provides a quantitative measure of individual customer satisfaction by asking customers to rate their experience on a scale or by using services such as BizRate, which samples your customers and rates your performance relative to industry standards	To detect systemic problems To reveal potential "land mines" that may negatively impact future financial performance

COMPUTER MODELS THAT PREDICT BEHAVIOR

There are a variety of techniques for modeling and predicting customer behavior. Some, such as collaborative filtering, have at times been billed as miracle cures that can be applied across a wide range of applications. But the truth is, no single technique works in all cases. The most successful models were developed by combining a number of different approaches to address the marketing objective at hand. Applied Predictive Technologies (APT) has developed a summary of the most commonly used techniques, how they work, and some associated online marketing applications (www.predictive technologies.com) (table 8-4).

Table 8-4 Computer Techniques for Modeling and
         Predicting Customer Behavior

Modeling Technique	How It Works	Associated Applications
Market basket analysis	Finds groups of items that tend to occur together in transactions	Cross-sell recommendations at checkout or with follow-up email
Collaborative filtering	Finds other users who share similar preferences with a target user	Affinity-based product recommendations in entertainment-oriented, multiple-SKU (product) environments
Cluster detection	Finds groups of users who are similar to one another	Create actionable segments of users for intermediate personalization and targeting (e.g., brand-conscious buyers receive a specific email solicitation)
Decision trees	Develops explicit rules to partition a data set into subsets	Product, content, and targeted advertising based on minimum click-stream data
Neural networks	Identifies generalized patterns in a training data set before seeking those patterns in broader data sets	Product, content, and targeted advertising based on large, heterogeneous, and incomplete click-stream and other data sets

Modeling Technique	How It Works	Associated Applications
OLAP	Multidimensional cross-tabulations of relational databases	Exploratory analysis Development of simple personalization rules
Regression	Statistical analysis of redundancy between data sets	Exploratory analysis Predictive variable identification
Generic algorithms	Applies replication, mutation, and natural selection to find optimal parameter settings for a predictive model	Optimize parameter settings to make the other techniques operate at peak performance

MEASURING RESPONSE DISTRIBUTION

If the average response rate (click-through) for an email marketing program is 15 percent, what is the response across the entire population of email recipients over the course of time? Is the same 15 percent group opening and responding to your messages every time? Is there a group of 25 percent of all recipients who are responsible for the majority of response activity? Or are your responses distributed equally across the entire population?

Say, for example, that over the course of a year you get a 10 percent average response rate across all email, but that the response is distributed over 75 percent of the recipients (the remaining 25 percent never respond at all). In the 75 percent group, then, people will respond to one out of every 7.5 emails they receive (10/75). On the other hand, if all your responses come from 30 percent of your recipients (with the other 70 percent never responding), each customer in the response group is responding, on average, to every third email (10/30). (These examples make the simplistic assumption that all responders do so with the same frequency. In real life, however, the actual distribution will be an exponential curve with a certain segment of customers being active responders while others respond infrequently.)

The chance that you'll deliver the right message at the right time will naturally be lower for infrequent responders than for frequent responders. If you discover that your recipients are only opening your messages 20 percent of the time, there is an 80 percent chance that they'll miss the most relevant message you deliver. Furthermore, if you can determine which subsets of your recipients have the lowest response rates, you'll probably want to perform a series of tests to try to figure out why they aren't responding and how you can improve your contact strategy to get them engaged.

MEASURING THE COST OF A CUSTOMER LOST

Sending irrelevant and poorly targeted email to customers is costly, not in offline terms of paper, printing, and postage, but in terms of something even more valuable: Every customer who disengages from an email marketing program is a lost opportunity to realize value from that customer in the future. If the customer disengages completely, the cost is relatively straightforward to calculate: It's what you've already spent on acquisition plus the expected future value of that customer. The expected future value of a customer is the life-time click-value (LTCV) of the customer minus the value you've already realized so far in your relationship with that customer.

It's a lot more difficult, however, to quantify the economic impact of a customer who is partially disengaged, or to understand and measure the factors that are causing that customer to give us only a portion of his or her attention.

One brick-and-mortar retailer was thrilled by the early responses to its email marketing program launch. Close to 40 percent of its customers clicked through on the initial emails. But within weeks, the response rate had tapered off to the high single digits. Customers still seemed to have some interest in the emails, but the initial enthusiasm had clearly waned. What was going on? Was the program still worthwhile? How could the retailer quantify the impact of being able to engage only a small fraction of its customers?

One way to gauge the cost of losing customers' attention is to evaluate the impact of email frequency and relevance on life-time click-value. This is a little harder than it sounds because neither frequency nor relevance are absolute measures but vary on a customer-by-customer basis. Let's assume that relevance is a function of individualization (targeting, timing, and personalization) and that there's no such thing as *too* relevant. But when it comes to frequency, there's no question that it's easy to reach the point of diminishing or even negative marginal returns (where each successive contact hurts more than it helps). While too much contact can be hurtful, too *little* contact can cause you to lose the customer's attention too. The difficulty is that the appropriate contact frequency is probably going to be different for each customer. Therefore one way to reduce contact frequency as a factor influencing customer value is to give customers a simple way to control how often they receive your emails.

So how can you tell when you're losing your customers' attention or when they're completely disengaging? Equally important, how do you measure the economic impact of losing that attention?

The brick-and-mortar retailer began to measure the correlation between the content of emails and customers' purchasing behavior. It discovered that its emails were indeed causing customers to buy more of the featured products. But this analysis did not indicate the missed opportunity and value of its disengaged customers. To understand this, the retailer would have had to take its analysis one step further and use the historical data it had already collected about its customers. Correlating the historical data about customers who had disengaged from the program with the increased value of customers who remained engaged would offer an indication of the potential economic value of reengaging the "lost" customers.

Problems with customer engagement can be detected by performing RFC analysis and contrasting it with contact frequency and relevance. Consider the following process for correlating customer engagement to your contact plan.

1. Select the customer segment you are going to analyze.
2. Select a time period over which you want to perform the analysis.
3. Graph the average RFC scores for that segment over the time period.

4. Evaluate the historical graph and determine whether there has been a change in (aggregate) RFC values (indicating a change in customer engagement).
5. Graph contact frequency and individualization for the chosen customer segment over the same time period.
6. Look for a correlation between level of engagement, contact frequency, and individualization.

These steps will enable you to correlate customer engagement with the email communications that have been designed to engage them. To estimate the cost of lower engagement, you need to recalculate the LTCV, which presumably will have decreased. The downward change in aggregate LTCV is essentially the opportunity cost of too much contact.

MEASURING YOUR RETURN ON LOYALTY

"Loyalty" is an overused and often loosely defined term. There have been several attempts to introduce a more precise financial definition of loyalty so that its impact on a business can be measured and quantified. In his book *The Loyalty Effect,* Frederick F. Reichheld does a superb job of describing the economics of loyalty by demonstrating the unquestionable financial impact of increased customer retention. Still, many people wonder whether loyalty programs actually work. Futhermore, when success is no longer driven exclusively by "cost of contact," we must be able to measure our "return on loyalty" related investments in order to determine the sucess of a program.

Netcentives (www.netcentives.com) has developed a Return on Loyalty (ROL) model, which measures the effect that a loyalty program has on a number of factors that all contribute to a customer's long-term value. The Netcentives model looks at increased conversion rates (sales that would not otherwise happen), increased lift (response rates higher than a baseline), impact on price erosion, and frequency of purchases, as well as other factors. Let's take a closer look at the ROL model.

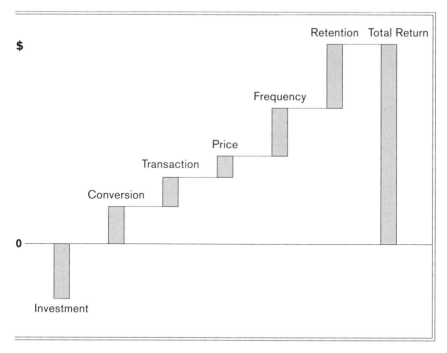

Quantifying the Return on Loyalty.

- *Investment.* Net present value (NPV) of total loyalty-related investments over the life span of a customer relationship
- *Conversion.* Incremental purchase activity as a function of increased loyalty
- *Transaction.* Lift as a function of loyalty program; generally a result of higher-margin product sold as a function of increased loyalty
- *Price.* Ability to maintain, not erode, price point as a function of increased loyalty
- *Frequency.* Increased number of purchases as a function of increased loyalty
- *Retention.* Increased life span of customer as a function of increased loyalty
- *Total return.* Gross returns on loyalty

To quantify the impact of your loyalty program you need to design a control group that doesn't receive loyalty rewards and compare results for the two different groups. This is a critical step because without a control group, it's impossible to precisely measure a program's loyalty-related impact and calculate the return on loyalty.

The Netcentives ROL model demonstrates how an increase in the value of a customer can be a function of programs that are designed specifically to improve loyalty. Netcentives operates "loyalty point networks" such as ClickRewards and AOL Advantage and therefore commonly uses points as the vehicle to drive increased loyalty. The ROL model nevertheless is applicable to any loyalty program regardless of the "currency" or mechanism used to increase customer loyalty.

INCENTIVES AND REWARDS, AND THEIR IMPACT ON LOYALTY

Imagine that you're walking down a city street when a complete stranger suddenly approaches you. He tells you he's just been transferred to a new position in Atlanta and has to move that weekend and asks if you'd be willing to help him load some boxes onto a truck. If you help him, he says, he's got a refrigerator full of cold beer that he'll share. Would you help? Would the incentive be enough? What if he said that he and his wife had planned a trip to Paris that they can't take because of the move and he'd be willing to give you a pair of airplane tickets?

On the other hand, what if you got a call from a friend who's making the same move and needs your help? You'd probably do it for nothing. She might give you a bottle of your favorite wine to show her appreciation. It's not really necessary, but it's still a nice reward.

Even though incentives and rewards tend to get lumped together, there's a big difference between the two. Incentives are ways to get people to do things they might not otherwise do. Rewards encourage and reinforce certain behavior. Used indiscriminately, though, rewards can often act like incentives and may even reinforce negative behavior.

Say, for instance, that exactly two weeks before the end of every fiscal quarter a company sends all its existing customers an email thanking them for their loyalty and offering them $10 off any purchase they make during the next week. The company may think it's rewarding customers, but as a reward this approach doesn't work. It may, in fact, have the negative effect of training customers to wait until the end of each quarter to make their purchases, knowing that they will receive a discount. A true reward, however, would be something—and it could be different for each customer segment—that's designed to reinforce certain behaviors. "Buy ten, get one free," is a reward. See Table 8-5 for a comparison of three different incentive and reward mechanisms and some common applications for each one.

Incentive and rewards programs can be very effective for acquiring new customers as well as for retaining existing ones. Frequent-

Table 8-5 Three Types of Incentive and Reward Mechanisms

Incentive and Reward Mechanisms	Description	Common Applications
Cash rebate: incentive in the form of cash refund or discount	• Effective incentive mechanism • Ineffective as reward mechanism • Minimal impact on loyalty • No cumulative effect (exception: cards such as Discover that give a rebate of the holder's annual charges. These programs don't engender loyalty to any particular product, but they do create an affiliation to the brand associated with the card.)	• Drive sales: 10% off on all merchandise • Push select merchandise through channel (inventory closeout, etc.) • "$100 cash" rebate on a specific product line: sell slow-moving inventory

Incentive and Reward Mechanisms	Description	Common Applications
Coupons: incentives and rewards delivered in the form of certificates containing restrictions on redemption	• Some can be collected and combined, but mostly used for one-time promotions • Some effect on loyalty as coupons can only be redeemed by issuer • Easily transferable	• Encourage current customer to make second purchase: "Receive $25 off next purchase of more than $100" • Cross sell: Amazon.com offers $15 coupon for purchases at Drugstore.com
Points: private "currency" that can be used to reward positive behavior	• Strong cumulative effect; people collect points • Strategic tool useful for influencing long-term behavior	• Discrimination: Selectively target emails and promotions based on point status • Recognition: Reach a certain point level and achieve special status and qualify for additional privileges (e.g., "Reach *United Executive Premier* status by flying 25,000 miles in one year")

flyer programs such as American Airlines' AmericanAdvantage are perhaps the best-known examples and have been tremendously successful. AAdvantage has moved from a simple loyalty program introduced to help American retain its best customers to a lucrative profit center. AAdvantage sells its points so that members can redeem them for all types of rewards, from rental car certificates to hotel vacations. AAdvantage points are even interchangeable with AOL Advantage points and can now be used for collecting rewards on AOL. In other words, they are turning into a currency for online shopping.

Other point programs have been designed with different goals in mind. With its focus on customer acquisition, MyPoints primarily offers companies incentives that they can give to new customers to attract their attention or get them to make a purchase. ClickRewards, on the other hand, gives online buyers the opportunity to collect points on purchases they make from a network of participating merchants building loyalty to the network participants. As we see, sometimes the line between rewards and incentives can get fuzzy.

If a customer gets an increasing number of points with each purchase from the same merchant (100 for the first, 120 for the second, 150 for the third, etc.), the natural inclination will be to keep buying only from that merchant. A well-designed rewards program increases the switching cost of your most loyal and valuable customers and greatly improves your chances of retaining them and of gaining an increased share of their wallet-and mind-share.

Email plays an important part in any loyalty and rewards program. Whether it is reaching out and offering promotional incentives to encourage new customers to make a purchase with you, communicating the status of your members' balances, or offering special redemptions to members who have reached a certain level, email is a powerful direct marketing tool for every loyalty program.

MEASURING THE SUCCESS
OF YOUR SERVICE PROVIDER

Whether an internal service group operates your email marketing program or you rely on an outside service provider, there's only one way to get accountability: Define clear success criteria. Let's take a look at some of the mechanisms you can put in place to evaluate the service organization responsible for operating your program:

1. *Define and monitor success criteria.*
   - Clearly articulate program goals and performance expectations.

- Agree on turnaround times for new programs, campaigns, or messages.
- Ensure that the service provider can be flexible and responsive to your ever-changing needs.
- Ensure that you understand what a service provider offers and what it expects others to provide and manage.

2. *Establish performance reviews.*
- Define agreed-upon milestones and time lines during implementation and operations.
- Set frequent (at least quarterly) performance reviews.
- Monitor performance of all participants (marketing, IT, customer service, e-commerce, outside service provider, etc.).
- Set up intradepartmental reviews to ensure that choice of service provider and/or technology solutions meets broader corporate goals and objectives.

3. *Demand performance and quality guarantees.*
- Establish service-level agreements with service provider.
- Evaluate quality of service history of service provider.
- Negotiate special performance guarantees for programs that have extraordinary demands (quick turnaround, high message volume, high degree of message personalization, unique data requirements and needs, etc.).
- Track the success of your programs over time in order to detect sudden or gradual shifts in performance or quality.

4. *Compare your results with industry averages.*
- Establish benchmarks based on comparable programs.
- Require that service provider presents its results relative to industry averages (to the extent that these can be identified).

5. *Monitor broader industry initiatives and developments.*
- Ensure that the service provider is keeping abreast of latest technology developments.
- Ensure that the service provider is keeping abreast of latest privacy legislation and its impact on your program.
- Demand guarantees that the provider is in good standing with major ISPs, privacy watchdog groups, and other email-related services (i.e., no spam complaints).

6. *Align your economic interests with your service provider's.*
   - Implement revenue-share models where appropriate.
   - Select a financial model and negotiate financial relationships that align your business goals with those of your service provider.

PART SCIENCE, PART ART—
AND GUIDED BY STRATEGY

One of the unique characteristics of doing business online is the ability it gives you to measure and track the success of your marketing programs. Yet success, as we have seen in this chapter, can be difficult to define. At the center is the continuous-feedback loop of tracking, measuring, seeking insight, and informing the program—a process based on both science and art. *Science* because we apply analytic techniques to the huge amounts of data and information in order to structure it and understand our customers' responses and behaviors. *Art* because lasting program success also depends on creative, out-of-the-box program design and interpretation inspired by the insight that we gather from the data.

When the marketers at eBags monitor the success of the My eBags email program, they focus on the numbers. They're tracking changes in month-to-month repeat purchase behavior that they can attribute to their email communications. The results are looking good, with over 33 percent repeat buyer growth within the program's first six months. At the same time, eBags is putting together a far broader perspective of its customers' future behavior by integrating customer service feedback, customer-driven product reviews, and member surveys with customers' transaction data and self-reported customer profiles. Coupled with a strategic, consumer-centric view of its business, eBags is leveraging this comprehensive customer knowledge to guide and shape its successful marketing programs.

The Internet provides marketers more data and hard results than ever before, yet the most difficult challenge is to understand what it all means. Measuring some things is easy: nobody's going to argue that 10 percent conversion to purchase from an email program is anything but phenomenal. But tracking your success over time, understanding and being able to quantify the factors that impact your program's long-term success requires patience, persistence, experience, and a lot of careful attention to the numbers. Sparks.com (www.sparks.com) the online service for buying real paper greeting cards, discovered that once a newly acquired customer opens an account originating from a sweepstakes, an email newsletter, or some other vehicle, the new customer will purchase Sparks greeting cards four times over the course of a year on average. Naturally, getting as many people as possible to give Sparks.com their email address is a key part of its success. Numbers such as these, phenomenal as they may be, don't just fly off the page. They require careful tracking of your customers' behavior. By making this investment, Sparks.com is now able to use the results to guide its marketing strategy and make informed decisions about how to effectively spend its marketing budget.

So who's going to dig up the gold in your data? Do you hire a team of analysts and let them figure out how to design, implement, measure, and analyze your Internet direct marketing programs? Or do you partner with service and technology providers to help you build your program? In Chapter 9 I address these questions as I describe who's who and how to think about putting all the pieces together.

WHO'S WHO?
PUTTING ALL THE
PIECES TOGETHER

WHETHER YOU'RE PLANNING to develop a full-scale, strategic Internet direct marketing program or simply trying to get your feet wet by running a few trial email campaigns, a number of questions probably leap to mind: How do I do it? Should I design it myself? Do I develop my own technology? Do I go to the traditional agencies my company has worked with in the past? Who has the expertise to help me design and execute my programs and campaigns? If the rules have changed, who understands the new ones?

The Internet direct marketing landscape is tough to navigate even for an insider. That's probably why there are so many service and technology providers out there, all claiming to offer the solution—or at least parts of it—to your company's total Internet direct marketing needs. But the solution that's truly most appropriate for *your* company depends on several things: your program requirements, your in-house marketing and technical expertise, your budget, and your corporate culture. This chapter will give the executive or manager charged with implementing your Internet direct marketing program a solid framework for understanding, categorizing, describing, and selecting vendors.

A FRAMEWORK FOR CATEGORIZING INTERNET DIRECT MARKETING PLAYERS

Unlike a traditional, direct marketing campaign, an Internet direct marketing program is a tightly integrated combination of marketing service, technology, and 24-7 operational support. Separating these three components by, for instance, engaging a marketing services group, building an in-house operations team, and purchasing off-the-shelf products is a definite possibility, but the lack of tight integration may limit the level of sophistication the program can achieve.

Internet Direct Marketing Program

Marketing services
24-7 operations
Technology platform + data

The layers of Internet direct marketing.

Chapter 7 described the required functionality of an email marketing technology platform or product, and Chapter 8 outlined how to measure the success of your service provider. This section focuses on evaluating the service and technology vendors you'll partner with to develop your programs. Having a framework for categorizing different vendors and service providers will help you select the best solution for your organization. The framework I propose (on the next page) breaks email marketing solutions into three separate dimensions: level of technical sophistication, level of marketing service, and operating model. The email marketing solutions grid was developed to evaluate service providers and vendors along two of the three dimensions: marketing services and technology sophistication. Given the rapid pace of change in the marketplace, there's no sense applying this framework to a limited number of specific companies that are offering email marketing solutions today. Instead, use this framework to help evaluate any company you're considering having a business relationship with.

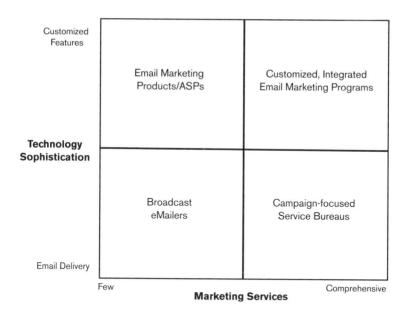

Email marketing solutions grid.

LEVEL OF TECHNICAL SOPHISTICATION

At the most basic level of technical sophistication are email broadcasters who send messages with little or no personalized content. This is essentially the online version of the direct mail model: buy a list and send the same piece of mail to everyone on it. There are some technical challenges associated with broadcasting very large volumes of email (50 to 100 million messages per day), but the solutions are generally fairly simple. If you need to deliver high volume (tens of millions at a time), such as "bulk" emails consisting of mostly text with little or no personalization, this may be the way to go.

On the other end of the technical continuum are the companies that send and track individual emails that are targeted, personalized, timed, and delivered to the right person at the right time. The focus is on data-driven communication with individual recipients. Say, for instance, that you purchase flowers from FTD.com. Three days later you get an (automatic) email with a tip for how to extend the life of the arrangement you just bought. To deliver the right message to the right person, the marketing system must keep track of a variety of data, including the shipping address of the flowers as well as the type of flowers delivered. These more advanced marketing technology solutions normally have Web-based application front ends that enable you to plan and execute programs, schedule new campaigns, target and personalize messages, perform testing and quality assurance, and access real-time reports. Applications such as these can also be customized to meet your marketing program's specific needs and can handle two-way, real-time, or batch data feeds. When mortgage rates fluctuate, iOwn has implemented real-time data feeds to their email marketing service provider so that emails can be delivered immediately to members who participate in the RateWatch program.

It's critically important to evaluate the technology solutions you're going to base your programs on. One very large online retailer who had worked with a number of different email marketing service providers recently switched to a new one who promised terrific technical features and functionality. It wasn't until after the retailer had already transferred its data and begun sending messages that it discovered some of the shortcomings of the new provider's technical platform. The platform couldn't, for example, maintain a complete history of customer interactions, which made it very complicated to target messages based on past response activity. Even worse, the retailer discovered that it couldn't import data from its retail stores and communicate with customers according to whether they shopped on the Web or in a store. This retailer is now considering a replacement provider and you can bet it's being far more diligent in its search.

Chapter 7 discussed how to evaluate the tools and technology of an email marketing program. Here a brief recap of some of the technology features you'll want to look for when choosing a technology platform.

- Full function application user interface
- Ability to implement customized marketing programs
- Support for individualized (one-to-one) communication
- Support for automated (triggered) communication

- Flexibility of underlying data models
- Data import and export capabilities
- Reporting and analysis capabilities
- Support for program testing and quality assurance
- Support for inbound email
- Integration with live profile pages

LEVEL OF MARKETING SERVICE

On one end of the service continuum are the broadcasters who simply merge the text copy you give them with a list of names and blast it out. Some may also provide such basic services as canned response reports to track click-through information. At the other end of the spectrum are the full-service marketing consulting and service bureaus. These companies run their clients' marketing functions in much the same way as traditional marketing and advertising agencies do. In Chapters 4 and 7, I discussed the different marketing services necessary to design and implement and email marketing program (developing a contact strategy/plan and implementing the message production process). Here are the services to look for when choosing a marketing service provider.

- Strategic marketing planning capabilities
- Campaign planning and execution capabilities
- Graphic design capabilities
- Copy writing capabilities
- Campaign or ongoing operations-based service model
- Data analysis capabilities
- Available partnerships

OPERATING MODEL

Your prospective vendor's operating model is perhaps the most important factor of all. There are a number of different ones to choose from, each with its own advantages and disadvantages. To evaluate the one that's right for you, you need to have a firm grasp on what it is that you're looking for. Maybe you're only looking to run a few campaigns to test whether email is right for you. Perhaps you want someone to analyze the results of a campaign you did in-house. Or maybe you are looking for a fully integrated email marketing program. Here are a few of the various models you have to choose from.

- *Pure marketing services.* These firms do consulting rather than actual campaign or program execution. They may, for instance, offer such services as analytical modeling, creative services, copy writing, campaign strategy, and brand development.
- *Product.* There are no services here, just software. You buy a product, get your IT organization to install it, develop an email campaign on your own (or hire a pure marketing service provider to assist you), and maintain the software and the programs yourself.
- *Application service provider.* The ASP delivers an email marketing software product as a service by hosting the product in a secure operating environment. You use the software over the Internet to plan, manage, and execute your email campaigns. This model normally needs some interaction with your IT staff to manage data transfers, but not all that much since your team won't have to install, maintain, or operate the software.
- *Marketing services and technology infrastructure.* The pure marketing services and ASP models combine to offer a completely outsourced email marketing solution. Using this model you can get basic support for designing and executing email campaigns or a fully integrated and customized email relationship marketing program. For most marketers, this is the most versatile model because you get the benefits of a specialized service provider who understands how to design, implement, and operate effective email marketing programs. The most advanced service providers also offer full access to campaign management tools and sophisticated reporting and analysis capabilities similar to those offered by pure product or ASP vendors.

If all you need is to send the same unpersonalized newsletter every week to a large group (millions) of recipients, you'll do fine with a basic email broadcaster. If you feel that you've got all the expertise you need in-house and are looking for pure product, you should be fine with a vendor offering an email marketing product or ASP. If you want a high level of specialized marketing service but don't need very sophisticated functionality, you can engage a campaign-focused service bureau. Finally, if you are looking for a high level of marketing expertise and service as well as a flexible, customizable technology platform that can support your program as its needs evolve toward greater sophistication, you will want to select a customized, integrated email marketing program provider.

WHERE TO TURN FOR HELP

A number of different providers can help you solve your email customer communications and marketing needs. Table 9-1 lists the most likely categories you have to choose from as well as a selection of a few relevant companies.

Let's take a close look at these categories.

EMAIL MARKETING SERVICE PROVIDERS

Over the past few years a new breed of company has grown up to meet the demand for complete solutions to companies' email marketing needs. Providers offer a wide variety of marketing services, technical capabilities, and focus. The services these companies (the three leading players are Post Communications, Message Media, and Digital Impact) provide range from customized email marketing programs and high-volume email delivery to one-off direct email campaign execution. Naturally, prices vary considerably. Most still charge based on the old direct marketing model of cost per email sent, while others have introduced new pricing models that are based on managing the customer database and optimizing the value of the client's customer relationships. What they have in common is that they allow you to outsource all—or at least a large part—of your email marketing solution.

Table 9-1 Email Marketing Services and Services Providers

Type of Service or Product	Sample Providers
Email direct marketing service providers	Post Communications, Message Media, Exactis (24/7 Media), Digital Impact
Email direct marketing ASPs and product companies	Responsys, Kana Communications
Opt-in list mailers and list brokers	YesMail (CMGI), NetCreations, Empower.net, DoubleClick, Flycast (CMGI)
Portals	Yahoo!, Excite, Lycos, AOL
Traditional direct marketing agencies	Impiric, Rapp Collins
Online agencies	marchFIRST, Razorfish, Modem Media Poppe Tyson, Agency.com Peppers and Rogers Group
System integrators	Viant, Scient, Organic Online
Specialty agencies/consultancies	Thread , Collaborate
Data modeling, profiling, and prediction	Personify, Netperceptions, Applied Predictive Technologies (APT), Datasage (Vignette), E.piphany
Inbound mail and instant messaging	Live Person, FaceTime, eGain, Brightware, Brigade

EMAIL MARKETING ASPS AND PRODUCT COMPANIES

A number of companies, including Responsys and Kava Communications, offer both stand-alone and hosted email marketing products. If you go with the ASP or product approach, your IT organization or a third-party systems integrator will have to implement and maintain your marketing program. The ASP greatly simplifies this process, since it handles installation, hosting, and configuration. Once the product has been implemented, your marketing organization must staff and train a team or hire an outside marketing services firm to operate the product in order to run your marketing program.

OPT-IN LIST MAILERS AND BROKERS

Some companies, such as YesMail and NetCreations, have built lists containing millions of opt-in email addresses. Others, such as Empower.net (formerly ALCi) act as list brokers and provide access to third-party opt-in lists. Opt-in mailers are focused on customer acquisition only. Because the quality of the lists these companies provide varies, it's absolutely essential that you know how often the people on the list you select have been contacted as well as the level of opt-in permission they gave. Banner advertising networks such as DoubleClick and Flycast (CMGI) have also moved into opt-in email, while MediaPlex has partnered with Post Communications and others to provide email direct marketing services. Among other things, they will subsidize newsletters for clients in exchange for the client allowing banner ads in the newsletters.

PORTALS

Microsoft, Yahoo!, and Excite operate new customer acquisition focused email marketing programs in conjunction with the free email service they offer on their sites. Users of Hotmail, Yahoo! Mail, or Excite Mail, for example, can sign up to receive special offers and discounts. Increasingly, portals will combine their broad view of their members' activities and interests with permission-based email marketing programs.

TRADITIONAL DIRECT MARKETING AGENCIES

Traditional direct marketing agencies such as Impiric or Rapp Collins do not currently provide email marketing services to their clients. They have, however, taken some initial steps to develop strategic partnerships with email marketing service providers so they can recommend preferred vendors when clients request them.

Because of the challenges involved in operating online, the new rules of Internet direct marketing will take a long time to permeate the traditional direct marketing mindset.

ONLINE AGENCIES

Online agencies such as marchFIRST, Razorfish, Modern Media Poppe Tyson, and Agency.com are well positioned to incorporate email marketing into the overall marketing services they provide to clients but have only recently started to do so. These agencies already understand the new discipline of e-marketing and are accustomed to moving fast, but they're a lot less experienced in direct marketing than the firms specializing in this field. Most online agencies are developing partnerships with email marketing service providers or technology providers as opposed to attempting to offer their own services.

SYSTEM INTEGRATORS

Companies such as Viant, Scient, and Organic can be called upon to build (expensive) custom, one-off email marketing solutions. It is unlikely that a company will want to implement an email marketing technology from scratch. Therefore, system integrators will primarily play a supporting role in email marketing and may partner with product companies and ASPs to assist clients who decide to buy email marketing packages. Alternatively, system integrators may partner with email marketing service providers to assist them in implementing and integrating customized programs. If a company has multiple customer information databases and would like to integrate the information into a single marketing data mart, it would use a data mart to run email programs and personalize content and offers on its website. A system integrator would probably be the right choice to perform this type of work. Since most of the integration work occurs around data transfers and database development, it's critical to make sure that they system integrators you're evaluating have proven database expertise. Some email marketing service providers will offer specialized system integration services to support the implementation and operations of their solutions and programs.

OTHERS

A number of players also offer products and services that are closely related to—and often should be integrated with—an email direct marketing solution. Peppers and Rogers Group (www.1-to-1.com) is growing rapidly as a global customer relationship management consulting group, specializing in helping organizations identify and implement *real* CRM initiatives. Thread (www.threadonline.com) is one of a number of boutique marketing services firms that specialize in developing a consistent brand experience online and offline. There are a host of technology-focused companies, such as Personify, Netperceptions, Broadbase, Applied Predictive Technologies (APT), Datasage (Vignette), and E.piphany, that provide profiling, data analysis, and prediction and recommendation tools and services.

Companies such as Live Person, FaceTime, eGain, Brightware, and Brigade also provide products, technology, and services for customer service, sales support, and handling inbound email and instant messaging. You must be prepared to communicate with your customers, whether they want to send you email asking a question, or use instant messaging to connect with a customer service or sales representative in real time. The integration of inbound email, instant messaging, and outbound email is a critical component of the fully integrated email relationship marketing solution. Look for email marketing service providers to forge close relationships with inbound mail providers (such as Brigade or Kana) and begin offering their own integrated inbound and outbound solutions.

OUTSOURCING VERSUS INSOURCING

Should your company build its own email marketing programs from scratch? Should you buy and install software products and hire and train your own email marketing staff? The answers may not be obvious. With the advent of a host of new Internet business models the real issue is whether or not you should outsource the entire operation to an email marketing service provider.

Traditional offline wisdom says that outsourcing happens late in an industry's life cycle. But online, it's just the opposite. Thanks to the Internet, there are a number of new models of technology and service outsourcing that can save your company time, resources, and money. Outsourcing critical business functions that are not part of your company's core competence has become the accepted way to rapidly expand your infrastructure and gain access to best-of-breed technology and service. It's beyond the scope of this book to get too much into the details of how, what, and why companies are outsourcing. Suffice it to say that the pervasiveness of the Internet and the resulting connectivity and easy access to computing resources is having a huge impact on the types of new services that can be outsourced. Outsourcing has very rapidly become a norm.

Some organizations are concerned that outsourcing will cause them to lose control. This is especially common in companies where IT has traditionally been responsible for supporting marketing's information needs as well as for implementing and operating the entire customer database. It's not entirely clear, though, why these companies are afraid of losing control. Sometimes they're worried about data security and the risks of hosting sensitive data on servers that are not controlled internally. Other times they're concerned they won't be able to add custom functionality or feature to a program.

Clearly, relying on an outside service provider will involve some risk. The service provider may lose important data because of poor backup procedures or substandard hardware and software. It may violate your customers' privacy rights by improperly sharing access to personal data. It may not be able to grow fast enough for your needs, making performance less than optimal. If you're considering outsourcing solutions be sure that prospective providers address your control issues so that everyone in your organization is comfortable with the decision to outsource.

All this goes to underscore just how important it is to carefully evaluate any potential service provider through due-diligence and reference checks. Leading outsourcers have probably encountered issues like the ones you are concerned about in the past, and they have undoubtedly developed appropriate responses to typical client concerns.

CONSOLIDATION AND INTEGRATION OF SERVICE OFFERINGS

Is email direct marketing an industry unto itself? Not at all. The principles of service-based marketing and communication outlined in this book are essential to the success of any online marketing initiative. And email is a mission-critical tool that plays an integral role in the e-marketing and communications mix for all online merchants. But as we've touched on earlier (and will discuss in greater detail in Chapters 10 and 11), email itself is just one of a large number of electronic communications channels that e-marketers will be using in the future. Furthermore, marketers ultimately won't want to manage relationships with a large number of different service providers.

That may be why there have been so many industry consolidations. Netcentives acquired Post Communications in order to broaden its technology infrastructure and provide a wide range of relationship marketing services, from customer acquisition programs and customized email relationship marketing programs to loyalty programs and promotions. In order to expand its service offerings to email broadcasting from integrated Web design services, 24/7 Media acquired Exactis.com. Kana acquired Connectify to be able to provide both inbound and outbound email products. In short, a number of different "constellations" are being formed to provide a rich suite of product and marketing services. And this is just the beginning.

The rapid move toward consolidation and the resulting increase in service offerings is going to continue at a frantic pace. I predict that the e-marketing landscape will be in a state of evolution for the first half of this decade. Growth opportunities in this industry are phenomenal and there is much more innovation and invention ahead of us than behind us. Broader global adoption of the Internet, new business models, new technologies, and the constant evolution of the e-marketing discipline itself will continue to fuel growth and consolidation.

EVALUATION CRITERIA

To end the "who's who" discussion, here is a summary of the most important criteria you should consider when making your final selection of a service provider or product vendor.

EVALUATE THE ENGAGEMENT MODEL

Ensure that your service provider can present you with a formal engagement model that contains tested processes and procedures that can take you from a defined marketing concept with clearly articulated goals and objectives to a fully operational email marketing service. Normally an engagement model will be broken into three main stages: design, implementation, and operation. When evaluating an engagement model, look for the following:

- A clear description of the stages that your service provider expects to lead you through, from program design to operational stability
- Formalized processes and procedures, for example, a kickoff process
- Design implementation, and operational guidelines containing expected resource requirements
- Quality assurance procedures
- Testing and disaster-recovery procedures

EVALUATE MARKETING SERVICES

Are the services your provider offers sufficient to meet your needs? Do they provide strategic oversight and guidance or are they focused only on tactical execution? Make sure the provider clearly defines the services it's offering and the level of participation and involvement your organization will need to operate a successful program. When evaluating a marketing services provider, look at the following:

- Services provided in-house as a core competency versus through partners and contractors

- Depth and breadth of services offered (domain experts versus generalists)
- Ability to select services (à la carte) versus fixed-service offering (take it or leave it)
- Flexibility to adapt to your organization's working style and culture
- Relevant reference clients (Go register with a couple of their programs and see what you get. Be clear about which parts the service provider is responsible for and which ones you'll have to handle in-house.)
- Makeup of account teams, including level of seniority and experience of team members

EVALUATE PROFESSIONAL SERVICES CAPABILITIES

Does your provider or product vendor have a professional services group or does it rely on your internal IT group or outside system integration services to install its product or integrate its technology platform? The quality of professional services groups varies widely and the vendor's own team is often not the one best suited to implement your email marketing solution. When evaluating professional services organizations, look for the following:

- An emphasis placed on professional services by the vendor (as opposed to your sudden realization that you need help implementing the vendor's solution).
- Depth and breadth of services offered.
- Detailed domain experience that maps to the problem your are attempting to solve and products or technology you have chosen.
- Composition of service teams, including level of seniority and experience of team members.
- If considering a third-party professional services firm, evaluate its experience working with the tools and technology vendor you have chosen. (You probably don't want to be their guinea pig.)

EVALUATE TECHNOLOGY INFRASTRUCTURE AND ARCHITECTURE

Pay close attention to your vendor's or service provider's product or technology architecture. How customizable is its solution? How scalable is the technology? Who are the people responsible for technology development and what are their credentials? When evaluating the technology infrastructure and architecture of a service provider or vendor, consider the following:

- What is the design philosophy underlying the technology or product? Is the technology or product intended for your type and size of business? Is it aligned with your marketing organization's philosophy?
- An Internet-based design center versus pre-Internet (client-server) design
- What is the history and evolution of the product? Did it "morph" into its current state or was it designed to be what it is from the beginning?
- Has the technology been around for a while or are you going to be on the "bleeding edge" by choosing this product?
- Does the feature-set map to your current needs and still leave room to grow?

EVALUATE OPERATIONS AND HOSTING INFRASTRUCTURE

If you are outsourcing the operations and hosting of your technology and data to a service provider you must carefully consider its operational infrastructure. Some service providers have built their own network operations and hosting centers, while others rely on third-party collocation services, such as Exodus Communications. When evaluating the operations and hosting infrastructure of your service provider, consider the following:

- The choices made for hosting and network operations
- The quality and reputation of possible third-party service providers such as collocation services

- System monitoring and failure-detection procedures (how quickly the service provider can detect that it is experiencing operating problems)
- Redundancy and disaster-recovery procedures
- Backup procedures and processes
- Network redundancy
- Geographic coverage

CHECK CLIENT REFERENCES

No one can give you a better indication of how well the product or service you're considering works than current and past customers or clients. Will the service or product provider offer all of its clients as references? If not, why not? Is it still doing business with all the clients on their client list? How does your company compare with the others on the list? Are you the same size? In the same business? Have the same industry focus?

EVALUATE OPERATING HISTORY AND PERFORMANCE

Ask the prospective service provider to outline its operating history. You want them to provide you with their service up-time as well as outline their operating procedures. The Internet is a very new place and an extra year or two of operations can make a big difference. Nothing beats the experience that 24–7 operations give a service company in terms of ironing out possible software bugs and streamlining operations. When evaluating operating history and performance, consider the following:

- How long the service provider has been in business
- The number of clients it services and how fast its business has grown
- History of catastrophic failures and client data loss
- Performance history for average and worst-case network congestion

PAY CAREFUL ATTENTION TO THE BUSINESS MODEL

How will your service provider or product vendor charge for its product, ASP service, or marketing service offering? There are several different business models in the market today, all with different benefits. Make sure you choose one that is aligned with the goals you've established for your marketing program.

Whether you decide that you should build your own Internet direct marketing solutions, purchase products, work with a service provider, or (most probably) choose some combination of the above, your success will depend on how deliberately you make your choices. If your internal IT group believes it should build everything, you probably won't be very successful—even if it reluctantly agrees to work with a service provider. If your marketing group wants to design and manage your programs but doesn't have the dedicated resources to do so, you'll be continually frustrated by the lack of activity in your programs and you'll probably end up with a product you're less than happy with. Understand and focus on your core competencies and bring in outside experts to help offload those areas that are not a core competence. As we move to the last section of the book, we set our sights toward the future of customer communication and Internet direct marketing. We'll start by considering how Internet direct marketing impacts your organization.

PART IV

LOOKING AHEAD

CHAPTER 10

THE ENGAGED
ORGANIZATION

A S WE LOOK TOWARD a future where companies routinely establish direct, individualized, and ongoing dialogue with thousands, hundreds of thousands, even millions of customers, it's getting increasingly clear that doing so will not only affect marketing departments but will actually influence the psychology and structure of entire corporations. Who owns and controls the dialogue with customers? Who manages relationships in the customer-centered organization? How do different departments and functions coordinate their efforts when communicating with customers? Orienting an organization around the customer is an absolute necessity for successful online commerce and marketing. Unfortunately, though, there are no simple formulas for how companies should organize and manage internal functions to address the new challenges that customer-focused marketing introduces. In short, the "engaged organization" is a work in progress.

This chapter looks at how companies—whether small home businesses, fast-growing dot-coms, or traditional brick-and-mortar operations—must get their organizations and departments ready to use the Internet to speak personally with each and every customer in order to maximize the long-term value of the organization's relationship capital.

MARKETING AS THE VOICE OF ALL CUSTOMER COMMUNICATION

If you want your customers to have a consistent experience and develop a loyal relationship with your brand, you must clearly define your organization's communications and relationship management responsibilities. Normally, marketing is responsible for managing an email direct marketing program, but it is not the only part of your organization that will engage with customers. Customer service, support, sales, and perhaps even e-commerce groups may also communicate with your customers independently.

To avoid any confusion, I propose that if your company is communicating with thousands, perhaps even millions, of customers, you put your marketing department in charge of managing and coordinating *all* customer communication, regardless of where it originates, and that the "relationship czar" discussed earlier be responsible for this initiative. Marketing's role in the engaged organization is to ensure that your company's email communication have a consistent voice, that they are focused on servicing the customer and effectively coordinated across all points of contact. To do this requires the following:

- Identify and define ownership and control of all customer communications functions
- Define interdepartmental guidelines, procedures, and processes for coordinating and managing customer dialogue
- Define objectives that align all departmental communications goals behind shared organizational interests
- Critically evaluate and streamline all responsibilities as they relate to customer dialogue

MARKETING AS A PROFIT CENTER

In most organizations, the sales department is responsible for revenue while marketing is a cost center, focused on brand building, product positioning, demand generation, and so forth. But when marketing becomes responsible for managing ongoing dialogue and building relationships with members, prospects, and customers, it also becomes responsible for a powerful alternative source of new revenue. It may not be appropriate for every organization to try to benefit financially from every connection with its members or customers, but for some it certainly won't hurt. In fact it can become a great service for their customers.

Palm, for instance, allows its third-party software and hardware developers to communicate with the Palm customer base through the InSync Online membership program. Developers can reach customers with highly targeted and personalized offers and information about the products and services they are selling. To the developers, InSync Online has proved to be a cost-effective way to communicate directly with an audience that has asked for relevant information. For the InSync Online member, the offers and information delivered by Palm are valuable, keeping them up-to-date on the exciting new products and services that are constantly being developed. Each InSync Online member specifies the categories that he or she is interested in and only receives offers and information in those categories. Palm charges developers for access to InSync Online members, and the revenue goes a long way toward offsetting the cost of operating the program.

When considering whether to make your email direct communications operation into a profit center, you need to factor in the nature of your business and the brand relationship your organization has with its customers. Victoria's Secret, for example, does not sell access to its customers. It decided that it would not permit any communication that could possibly dilute the Victoria's Secret brand relationship. As a result, when customers give Victoria's Secret permission to communicate with them by email, they are confident that they'll be hearing *only* from Victoria's Secret and not from anyone else. In fact, customers may well consider it a breach of trust if they suddenly began to receive emails "brought to you by Victoria's Secret" with offers from other companies.

One of the dangers of a cost-effective, rapid-reaction tool such as email is that it can easily be used to realize short-term revenue goals rather than to maximize long-term performance, compromising your company's customer relationships in the process. Imagine for a moment that your sales organization is not meeting its quota for the quarter. It might be tempted to use email to broadcast a special offer to all your customers designed to squeeze another round of sales out of them. While even relatively low response and conversion rates can bring in significant revenue, a knee-jerk program like this will probably compromise your goal of building a lasting dialogue with your customers. A small percentage will probably buy something, but the rest will experience the message as annoying and irrelevant.

In the engaged organization, your sales organization's goals must be aligned with your corporate goals of maximizing the long-term value of your customer base. Although every sales organization will have quotas, it should be evident that pitting short-term tactics against long-term goals is a decision you need to make very carefully.

MARKETING IN A WORLD OF NEW CUSTOMER EXPECTATIONS

Forget thinking about your role as a marketer as a day job. When your website is up, or you send out an email, customers expect you to be open for business. They expect to be able to tell you what they want and get a response right away. The engaged organization actively communicates with and responds to customers 24 hours a day, 7 days a week. And real time is the only time. As the marketing function moves away from the onetime campaign focus of the past to the continuous communications focus of the Internet, the new marketer has to be able to demand real-time access to data, information, and results. To be successful, online companies are trying to support the new demands of 24-7 marketing—and the effects are rippling across entire organizations. Here's what customers expect and the impact of these expectations on your engaged organization.

THE INTERNET ENABLES NEW FORMS OF COLLABORATION

Thanks to the Internet, organizations now use the Web to collaboratively share and access information internally and externally without regard to physical location or time. In addition, service organizations have developed Web-based tools that enable them to interact with clients in real time while planning, executing, and tracking their marketing programs.

Laura, an account manager at the email marketing service firm responsible for the Palm InSync Online program, was on the road when she received an urgent message that Palm needed to send out an immediate email to their InSync members. They were about to announce an exciting new product and realized that notifying their InSync members slightly ahead of the general announcement would be a good idea, giving their loyal customers a heads-up so they, in

Customer Expectations	Organizational Impact
If the website responds, you're open for business.	24-7 operations and staffing
If I've signed up with you and I send you an email, I expect you to know who I am.	Integrated view of customer across traditional organizational boundaries
I expect you to respond promptly to my inquiries and requests.	Cross-functional policies and goals governing response times
You'll contact me only if you've got something worthwhile to say.	Integrated customer profiles that span functional boundaries
You won't bombard me with email.	Central gatekeeper controls and limits all outbound communication
You'll respect my privacy.	Privacy and information use policy that applies to all parts of the organization
You'll make it easy for me to access information pertaining to things I care about.	Links between all internal and external services (email, website, webstore, phone center, UPS, Fed Ex)
If you send me a personal email, you know who I am no matter how I respond (via telephone, Web, email, or in person at a retail outlet).	All customer "touch points" have access to customer profiles

turn, could spread the word. From her hotel room somewhere in Chicago, Laura used her laptop computer to log on to the email marketing tools her firm has developed to run programs such as InSync Online. She loaded the message, targeted it to the appropriate member segments, performed an automated quality test, then got on the phone with the client and asked him to approve the message. Once she had the thumbs-up, Laura scheduled the message for midnight delivery and went to bed. The next morning she logged on again to run a report of the response the message was generating and emailed a copy to Palm. Not only had Laura remotely administered the message; she had coordinated and validated her efforts with the client in real-time—all on the Web.

REDRAWING ORGANIZATIONAL BOUNDARIES

In January 2000, Forrester Research advocated that companies "merge marketing and customer service into one department." Why? Because dialogue implies a continuous back-and-forth, where both parties talk and both listen. Yet today most companies organize their inbound and outbound functions separately. To avoid this, the engaged organization must organize all its marketing, customer service, and support functions into one department. This way, customers visiting the company's website or receiving email see a single company and a single brand.

There are two primary reasons why it makes sense to combine customer service support and marketing into one department. First, organizing different functions under the same department lets you align their goals and measures of success. When the goal is to build and nurture lasting relationships by engaging customers in an ongoing dialogue, it makes intuitive sense that the inbound and outbound parts of that dialogue come from the same place. Second, most organizations with separate customer service and marketing departments use information systems that probably don't communicate with each other. This means that marketing doesn't know a customer's status with customer service. Is he happy and satisfied or miserable and angry? Could she possibly be turned into a spokesperson for your company? Combining information from different parts of your organization to give you a real-time snapshot of your customers will make your customer communication programs far more effective.

An interesting exercise that can help you understand how organizational boundaries impact customer communication is to identify the parts of the organization that interact with the customer at each stage in the customer life cycle. For instance, which parts of your company are involved in leading a prospect or customer from interest to actual purchase? If the customer receives a highly relevant email from your marketing department and decides to engage, does your website provide him with a pure, self-service experience from there or can he get help in the buying process? What if he has questions while visiting the website—can he connect with a real person and get them answered immediately?

Another boundary you may want to redraw is the one between your marketing and technical departments. Most companies have problems getting their marketing departments and technical teams to communicate with each other effectively and regularly. During my work with Post Communications we frequently discover that a client's technical people will talk to Post's technical people, who in turn talk to Post's account manager. The account manager then speaks with the client's marketing contacts. In other words, the client's technical and marketing people frequently have no forum for meeting and communicating. To address this issue, weekly meetings between account managers and technical project managers and the client's technical and marketing teams are essential. This has been an incredibly effective way of improving communications.

ANOINTING A "RELATIONSHIP CZAR"

As we've discussed previously, every engaged organization needs a "relationship czar"—a relationship marketing manager—who is responsible for the integrity of the relationship the organization develops with its members and customers. At Homestore.com, the person responsible for email direct marketing has a deep background in traditional direct marketing, having spent a significant part of his career at American Express, an acknowledged leader and innovator in offline relationship marketing. He brings extensive experience to his responsibility of coordinating outbound customer and member communication across all of Homestore.com's properties, including SpringStreet.com, REALTOR.com, and Home-Fair.com. Homestore.com's goal is to recognize, reward, and respond to members across all its properties, assisting them with their all home-related needs. Homestore wants its customers to understand that whether they're renting a new apartment, buying their first home, applying for a new mortgage, or redecorating their homes, the company is there for them. It will be able to achieve this goal only if it recognizes and communicates with its members across all properties and over their entire life span with Homestore.com.

Although relationship czar is normally a marketing position, the job responsibilities clearly span traditional organizational boundaries, with broad oversight responsibilities for all points of customer contact. Whether a customer drops by a retail store, calls the 800 number to place an order or ask a question, returns a product, visits the website, receives an email, or is contacted by regular mail, the relationship marketing manager is the one who ensures that the organization recognizes the customer and speaks with a single, consistent voice. In a sense, the relationship czar is the internal spokesperson and voice of the customer. Whenever the organization is planning a new program that includes customer contact, the relationship czar acts as the "proxy customer" and should be consulted.

CUSTOMER COMMUNICATIONS MANAGEMENT (CCM): A NEW DISCIPLINE

Juggling and managing the many aspects of communicating with customers is a significant intraorganizational challenge, so significant that it really warrants its own label. I propose using the term customer communications management. CCM looks at centralizing the communications function while making it possible to keep existing organizational structures in place.

The accompanying diagram illustrates how an organization's broader customer communications requirements would be handled under a CCM scenario. Every part of Company X (such as marketing, sales, e-commerce and customer service) that has direct contact with a customer must funnel its contacts through a "customer communications gateway," which is managed by marketing. That way, all of the organization's direct customer contact remains controlled by the same department. With a full-fledged CCM plan in place it allows you to communicate with your customers the way they want you to—whether by phone, email, or even regular mail. You don't, of course, have to implement your CCM initiative across all channels before you get going. Integrating all of your email contact is a great place to start.

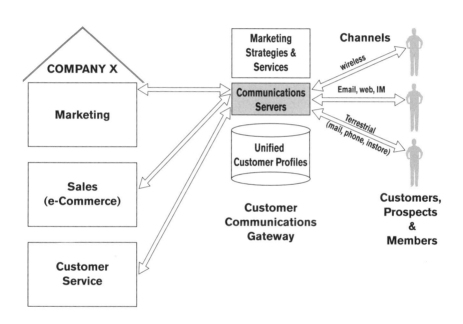

Customer communications management (CCM).

The advantage to your customers of the CCM model is that they experience a single, unified voice. They are less likely to receive five messages one week and then nothing for the next month. If you have a CCM-based relationship with a customer, you'll know, for instance, if she's sent an email to customer service. Until her question has been resolved, no marketing or promotional contact will occur. If a customer sends you an email asking a question or expressing a complaint, the last thing she wants is some kind of promotional offer. If this happens, she's likely to think that you're not listening. Would she be wrong?

Imagine that you just bought a new, digitally remastered Louis Armstrong CD from CDNOW as a result of an email they sent you. As soon as you make your purchase you instantly receive a confirmation email that includes an offer to buy another CD, this one with Louis Armstrong and Ella Fitzgerald performing together. One click on the link in the confirmation email and this CD is added to your order. Or imagine exchanging emails with a retailer about a purchase that was damaged when it arrived. In the final email the retailer confirms that your replacement has been shipped. It also contains a message thanking you for your patience, apologizing for the inconvenience, and offering you 20 percent off your next purchase. These are both examples of how marketers can put programs in place to automatically append information to the standard e-commerce and customer service responses as the message travels through the customer communications gateway.

Implementing CCM involves both a technical solution and an organizational initiative. As with email direct marketing (which is a subset of CCM), it's possible to build your own CCM solution; alternatively, you can outsource it to a service provider. If you're considering this option, you will, of course, need to get buy-in and participation from every part of your organization that has direct contact with your customers.

While combining marketing and customer service into a single department may be the right thing to do for the customer, it may be impossible for your company to do anytime soon. The principles of CCM apply nevertheless and can be implemented as long as you have organizational commitment to sharing customer data between the systems and services your departments use.

CCM is related to—but different from—another important field: customer relationship management (CRM). I have deliberately not discussed CRM in this book; it has actually been around for a while, but has been so broadly defined that it has come to mean very different things in different industries. Depending on how you and your company define CRM, you may want to consider making CCM a part of your CRM strategy. CCM may also be a way to begin implementing a CRM initiative. Over time, the CCM function will become more critical. The need to fully integrate customer communications across organizations will only become more pronounced as organizations engage their customers in individualized dialogue.

SIZE MATTERS

Every organization, large or small, can use email to establish a dialogue and build loyalty among its prospects, members, and customers. And every organization, regardless of size, needs to follow the guidelines and principles outlined in this book. But size *does* matter when it comes to the investment a company can make in infrastructure and the number of people it can commit to developing and operating a program. Don't worry, though. Even small businesses with limited resources have plenty of ways to use email to communicate with their customers.

If your company has only a small number of customers or clients, you may still be able to use your regular email software to send out messages, announcements, and newsletters. This type of program ends up looking a lot like the regular email dialogue you would have with your customers or clients. You send out a message to your client list and respond to their requests individually. The advantage is that you can establish a very personal dialogue with every client. However, this solution works only for a small client base, and even maintaining infrequent communication can take up a lot of time. Fortunately, there are several basic software packages that can help you maintain simple mailing lists and send broadcast emails to your lists. L-Soft's LISTSERV product, Responsys, and Message Media's RevNet are just three of these. At the point where your organization starts running its own mailing list, a marketing person and an IT person will need to begin dedicating significant amounts of time to managing the program.

Working with an email marketing service provider is probably not going to be a viable option for very small businesses: it's hard to justify the level of investment necessary to develop a customized program if it's going to support only a few hundred or perhaps even a few thousand customers. That said, service providers who focus on the small business market will probably surface in the near future. They'll offer basic, turnkey email marketing and customer communications services at a much lower cost than today's higher-end service providers.

Also, there will probably be more advanced products available on the market over the course of the next few years that will enable smaller companies to communicate with up to a few thousand customers in a personal manner by setting up and organizing their own small customer databases. These developments mean that large organizations aren't the only ones who need to think about the organizational impact of continuous customer communication. Any organization that needs to stay in touch with its customers—and that means every business—will be impacted as well.

LISTENING TO AND LEARNING FROM YOUR CUSTOMERS

When an electronic products company started its email marketing program, it quickly discovered that it had a lingering problem with dissatisfied customers. The company had promised a free giveaway as an incentive to get customers to register their product. But due to a problem with the fulfillment house, the gifts were not sent out on a regular basis. A number of customers who were annoyed that they hadn't received their free gift began taking advantage of email to talk back to the company. The company had had no previous direct contact with these—or any other—customers and didn't even know that the problem existed. Needless to say, the company now pays careful attention to its inbound email and also runs frequent surveys as ways to listen and learn from its customers.

Becoming a listening and learning organization may require a cultural adjustment, but most companies can achieve a lot by implementing these simple business procedures, which focus on capturing information and data from all customer interactions. Let's take a brief look at some of them.

1. *Establish cross-departmental distribution of customer feedback.*
   Listening to your customers means that everyone in your

organization must be able to hear what they're saying, whether they work in the technology group, marketing, customer service, merchandising, or elsewhere.

2. *Provide easy, online access to all campaign results and customer satisfaction reports.* You may choose to implement a Web-based application that allows appropriate people across your organization to access a weekly customer status report, or you may email it around to everyone. Either way, the input and results provided by your customers should inform and govern the way a broad section of your organization thinks.

3. *Tie customer satisfaction to employee reward and compensation.* High customer satisfaction may mean that you can hire more personnel, get more resources for your project, or even compensate yourself and your employees better. Making customer satisfaction—not just revenue—matter sends a powerful message to your customers.

4. *Tie customer loyalty and long-term value to employee reward and compensation.* Although customers may like something they bought, are they coming back to buy again? If you tie both loyalty and long-term value (as well as customer satisfaction) to employee compensation you'll create a culture that understands that you don't just need happy customers—you need happy customers who generate lots of value.

THE ROLE OF IT IN A
GLOBALLY NETWORKED WORLD

As we discussed in Chapter 1, the Internet ties all information systems together regardless of their physical location. In effect, it has enabled a company's internal computer network, its local area network (LAN), to extend its reach on a global scale. Organizations are therefore no longer constrained by the information systems they can build or buy and install on their own physical premises. Every computer is connected to every other computer on the Internet. This simple truth changes everything. What used to be "internal computing resources" at a company have now become external resources that the engaged organization makes available to all its constituents. The reality of the Internet is that everybody is connected to you and you are connected to everyone else: your customers, your vendors, your suppliers—even your competitors. It doesn't matter where a particular network function is physically located or who operates it, just as long as it's secure and reliable and provides the right functionality to solve a particular problem.

In the old days of client-server computing, the classic model for adding new functionality to your corporate network was to purchase server hardware and software—complex, heavily specialized systems which the IT department would have to install, operate, upgrade, and maintain. If, for instance, your marketing people requested new functionality that would allow them to access information in the central customer database (assuming that the organization had one), you'd probably have to buy and install new servers and customize your software. You'd also need to install specialized client software on the desktop computers you were planning to use to access the information. And, of course, all this software would need to be maintained and frequently upgraded. Maintaining such seemingly simple solutions could be incredibly expensive.

Today, the engaged organization looks to the network for solutions to its information technology needs. Accounting, sales, marketing, and many other services are available online, hosted and maintained by various service providers. As a result, adding new functionality to a company's network is becoming a function of selecting the right service provider. The benefit: A department such as marketing no longer needs to wait for IT to install or build its own technology solution. Instead, it can get outside support.

IT's role in an engaged organization is still to develop and manage the mission-critical core components of an organization's technology infrastructure, but it also includes an equally important yet very different set of responsibilities: IT must evaluate, help select, and support a variety of virtual resources, all of which are hosted and operated by outside service providers on the network. Much of the work in supporting these virtual resources involves coordinating data flow and ensuring data security and consistency across all network services.

Imagine that you want to use the 350,000 email addresses in your customer database to develop an email marketing program. The traditional company would approach this in terms of software and servers. It would ask what software and how many servers were needed to deliver 350,000 emails to its customers. The engaged company would ask very different questions: Which service provider on the network can accept an automated data feed from our customer database? Can the service provider design, deliver, and track—on an ongoing basis—a personalized email campaign and monitor the complete history of our interactions with every individual customer? And finally, can we get "phase one" built and launched in two weeks?

In Chapter 1, I suggested that we need to take business back to the way things operated a hundred years ago, to a time when several new technologies—the railroad, the automobile, and the telephone—disrupted traditional ways of doing business. They also enabled the growth of retailing as we know it today. Today, the Internet is having a major impact on the way companies conduct their business and structure their organizations. The disruption caused by Internet technologies is enabling us to reintroduce some of the benefits of the personal relationships we once had with neighborhood storekeepers.

How customer marketing and communication impacts your organization is something you'll have to manage by restructuring your traditional organizational functions and by leveraging the new infrastructure and new technologies. Although reorganizing, reorienting, and refocusing an organization almost always involves some pain, you really don't have a choice. Online customers have learned to expect the companies they do business with to recognize and integrate their actions across all systems, divisions, departments, and functional groups. When customers tell you something, they expect you to listen and respond promptly. They also expect you to remember what they've told you in the past and to take that into consideration the next time they interact with you. If you don't engage with them on these terms they won't engage with you. If you do, they'll give you exactly what you want: their repeat business and loyalty.

Existing organizations and traditional structures are already being strongly impacted by the ideas we've discussed in this book. In Chapter 11 we'll look at how changes in the not-so-distant future will affect how customers buy products and companies market, service, and sell them. As we shall see, the boundaries between marketing, servicing, and selling become nearly indistinguishable. Fasten your seatbelt; things in your company may already be changing faster than you ever imagined, but it's only the beginning of the ride.

THE FUTURE OF
CUSTOMER DIALOGUE

THUS FAR I HAVE focused on email's value as an immensely efficient tool that companies can use to build an ongoing dialogue with their customers. While email is here to stay, the future of customer dialogue will rapidly expand far beyond anything we know today. Individualized communications delivered to customers via websites, instant messaging, and wireless devices are just the very beginning.

The Internet will be everywhere in the future. It will become a part of the very fabric of all communication and almost all devices, ranging from your car to your home, to your sprinkler system. Your cellular telephone will be connected to the *network*. (More on that shortly.) Some companies, such as Amazon.com, already have websites that recognize customers every time they return. Amazon's patented one-click functionality is based on knowing who you are; a single click then triggers its system to pull up all the pertinent information they have about you, complete your purchase, and ship your order. This functionality is also available on the Palm VII wireless handheld computer, making it possible to buy a book from Amazon.com wherever you are.

Some online retailers have begun to use instant messaging as a way to engage their customers in real time. Shoppers at the Land's

End website, for example, can reach real, live people through the site's instant messaging function, ask questions, search for products, find the right size, and even get help as they go through the screens that lead to the final purchase. And as the Internet becomes so pervasive that it becomes part of the background, organizations will engage with their members and customers in ways that haven't even been discovered yet.

EXPECT THE INTERNET TO BE EVERYWHERE

As I write this at the beginning of the year 2000, there are ten taxicabs in San Francisco that are painted bright purple and yellow and sport a big Yahoo! logo. Each has a computer onboard that offers customers wireless Internet access. For no extra charge you can browse the Web, check your email, trade stocks, order your groceries, look up directions to a restaurant or bar you'll be patronizing that evening, and so on. Within a couple of years, every cab in San Francisco will have Internet access.

Otis Elevators recently announced that it would begin equipping elevators with Internet access. As passengers ride up and down to their offices, hotel rooms, or meetings, they will be able to read the latest news, check the stock market, or take a quick look at the website of the company they're about to visit.

With the rapid industry adoption of standards such as wireless access protocol (WAP) and wireless markup language (WML), cellular telephones will soon all have built-in Internet access. Some already do: The Neopoint cell phone uses a built-in microbrowser to allow users to surf to their heart's content. Imagine that you've got a retail store and someone comes in with a Neopoint phone and starts looking up products on the Web using a price comparison service. If he finds what he's looking for but doesn't like your price or service, he'll just order it online from someone else—right from your store. Even cooler, this device greatly improves the way you access your voice mail and email services. When combined with a service from Onebox.com (a Phone.com company, which provides free voice mail, email, and fax through a Web-based universal mailbox), Neopoint becomes your wireless communications center.

And whether you're in the back seat of a San Francisco cab, in an Otis elevator, or talking on the phone, you can take advantage of a service offered by LastMinuteTravel.com. If you've told them you're interested in last-minute weekend getaways, they'll send messages directly to your Internet-connected wireless phone with time-sensitive offers for hotel rooms, airline tickets, and more. Who knows, you might just want to send an email from the elevator canceling your appointment and take that cab right to the airport.

Sound extreme? You ain't seen nothing yet. The Internet is going to have a less obvious and possibly even more powerful effect as it starts to connect the devices we rely on every day of our lives, such as dishwashers, sprinkler systems, and automobiles. You can already buy a car that has a wireless connection or a satellite link to the Internet. General Motors has established a partnership with Qualcom and America Online to build 400,000 cars with Web access this year. In Japan, you can buy a car that will read your email for you as you drive to work in the morning.

Imagine that it's late spring and you're driving up to a ski resort for the weekend. The snow is melting and by the time you get home Sunday night, your car is a mess—covered with mud and a thin layer of salt. When you check your email the next morning, there is a message from your local car dealer with an offer for a complete detailing job, including a special underbody rinse designed to remove salt and protect your car from corrosion. The email also asks if you are planning any more ski trips this season. If not, the dealer would be happy to remove and wash your ski rack as part of the detailing job. Was the timing of this offer a coincidence? Absolutely not.

When you bought the car, the dealer asked for your email address and whether you would like to sign your new car up for a service that would monitor its performance, notify you when it was ready for service, and alert you about additional features. It won't be long until global positioning system (GPS) devices in your car will keep track of where you go for the weekend and relay this information to your local dealer's customer database (with your permission, of course). Knowing that the mountains had spring weather conditions, dealers could run a program that automatically sends an email offer to anyone who drives to the mountains. Since they would know that your car has a ski rack, the offer to help remove it would be automatically added to the email.

If your dishwasher or garden sprinkler system is on the Internet, they can "notify" their manufacturers if they break or need maintenance. And just to cover all the bases, as a service to customers, manufacturers will monitor their appliances and send instant email if they need repair or maintenance. If your sprinkler system is set to go off every day during the rainy season, the manufacturer might even send you an email suggesting that you change your watering schedule and offering simple instructions for how to do it. The company might even be able to do it for you by remote, using its Internet connection to control your system. As devices and products of all kinds become linked to the network, manufacturers gain a powerful new way to connect with their customers. Successful organizations will use these additional connections as opportunities to provide new services and establish dialogue with their customers.

THE TELL-ME-MORE TELEVISION

Most currently available interactive television technologies are nothing to get excited about. They've all been variations on the movie-on-demand and pizza-to-go themes. The problem, of course, is that we already have movies on demand: you rent them at the local video shop. And we have pizza to go: just pick up the telephone. But what if the boundary between television and the World Wide Web blurred? What if you really could tell your TV what you were interested in and it would find it for you?

Imagine that you're watching the news one evening when your interest is piqued by a story about the United States awarding most-favored-nation trading status to the People's Republic of China. You want to learn more, so you click on the Tell Me More button on your television screen. Several icons appear superimposed on the images you're watching. Movie icons ("micons") display recent related stories from a video library, and there are links to several recent print stories as well. There is a promotion to buy a music CD from a new hot rock group from Beijing and a link to a travel service that specializes in Chinese travel. Click on one of the micons and you can view that story you missed on the Tienanmen Square uprising expanding on the connection between trade status and human rights. The news story on the television pauses and the Tienanmen video clip begins to play. As it unfolds, additional micons and story links appear on the screen, allowing you to dig deeper and learn more. You decide to watch the full story. When it's over, you return to the original newscast—right where you left off. Back at the most-favored-nation story, you click on a couple of print story links as well as the travel link, sending the information directly to your email box.

Later that same evening you're watching one of your favorite shows (with no commercials, of course) when your television tells you that you just reached the "platinum viewer status" for this show. From now on you'll receive 25 points for every product that you request information about and 2 points for every dollar you spend on those products. As usual, everything in the show is for sale, from the furniture to the music—even the clothes the actors are wearing. Just click on the Tell Me More button and information on the items you're interested in is automatically emailed to you. One of the items you requested information on was a car. When you check your email you find that your local dealer has delivered something: it's not an advertisement, though; it's a calendar for scheduling a test drive and a summary of your lease and trade-in options.

Whether you like it or not, this isn't some far-fetched science fiction fantasy. MIT's famous Media Laboratory has performed demonstrations of various forms of tell-me-more televisions for over a decade. The technology and infrastructure for making your computer, cell phone, car, and television a part of the global Internet is either here today or waiting just around the corner. Whether the particular scenarios above appeal to you or not isn't important. As technology advances, so do the opportunities for interactive customer dialogue. It will take a while for the principles of interactive dialogue to catch on broadly, but it's not too early to start planning for the future. If you put your customers in the driver's seat and listen, learn, respect their privacy and focus on service, you'll win their hearts, their minds, and their loyalty. And by doing so, you'll be laying the groundwork for becoming a truly engaged organization of the next decade.

PRIVACY NIGHTMARE OR SERVICE DREAM?

So what becomes of our individual privacy and anonymity in a world where there is an Internet-ready device at every turn we make. Aren't we being bombarded with enough information and advertising as it is? Are car manufacturers going to "eavesdrop" on our weekend getaways? And who's going to know that I rode an elevator in Chicago last Thursday afternoon? Is "somebody out there" going to know every TV show-watch? Are we marching toward a privacy nightmare or a service and convenience dream? What is going to keep the car manufacturer from selling your whereabouts to other vendors, or even letting it fall into the hands of sophisticated robbers who could drop by your house while you're spending the weekend in the mountains?

The potential of all these technologies is endless and so is the potential to abuse it. That's why the federal government needs to step in and proactively write comprehensive privacy legislation. Consumers must be given full control over their personal information including the ability to review, modify, or delete all information stored about them. At the same time, the goal should not be to control and dictate how organizations use the information they collect (beyond the obvious need to protect the privacy of children, for example). Instead, legislation needs to be focused on organizations' ability to collect and use information without the explicit approval and awareness of their customers and members. (We discuss privacy legislation in greater detail later in this chapter.) Only by requiring companies to comply with opt-in and full-disclosure principles can we realize the potential of new and exciting services.

What engaged companies are realizing is that privacy is not some heavy burden that they should consider a threat. On the contrary, it's good for business. A privacy orientation builds *relationship capital* through the trust it establishes with customers. It forces your organization to focus its systems and procedures on the customer. It maintains brand equity by avoiding the negative feelings and publicity associated with privacy violations and it demonstrates leadership. Finally, and most important, it is the right thing to do by your customers.

EXTENDING YOUR CUSTOMER'S EXPERIENCE OF DIALOGUE THROUGH NEW TECHNOLOGIES AND CAPABILITIES

Back to the car of the future—the one with the Internet connection and onboard GPS system. Car manufacturers will no longer be just in the business of making and selling cars. In fact, that could end up being the smallest part of their business. If it were up to GM, they'd establish a relationship with you to service all your car transportation needs. They would pick up your car once a week and have it cleaned. They would offer you a car if you needed to travel to a different city and, of course, they would have someone pick up and deliver your car curbside at the airport. They would finance your car and, naturally, service it. They would even offer you the seasonal car program providing a convertible during the summer and an all-wheel-drive in winter. They would engage you in a dialogue that would make owning and using your car easier and more convenient. In the future when you buy a car you will also be able to sign up for a reward program that gives you points when you make your lease payment on time, when you get your car serviced by an authorized provider, or when you make a purchase from any company participating in the program. As you leave the ski area on Sunday evening, your on-board computer pings, offering you a certificate for 100 points the next time you buy lift tickets at a participating ski resort. With the touch of a button, you forward the offer to your email box where you can retrieve it the next morning. On the drive home, your GPS map screen occasionally lights up and tells you in a soft voice about things you may be interested in along the road. If you want to bookmark anything, you just push a button on the dashboard and forward the information to your email address. As your fuel level gets low, your car tells you when the next gas station is coming up. But not just any gas station—the computer knows to notify you about gas stations that are participating in your rewards program. (If there is no participating gas station in the area and you're about to run out of gas, the service you've signed up for will, hopefully, direct you to the closest available gas station.)

Although these services are still in the future, shorter-term technology developments and new levels of systems integration can enhance customer dialogue in a number of exciting ways.

EMAIL

The greatest short-term impact is happening as a result of HTML email—the ability to send and display web pages in an email program. Close to half of all Internet users can now receive HTML email and this number is growing every day. With active web pages delivered by email, it is fast becoming possible to interact with customers directly from within the message. Questions and forms allow recipients to submit answers and additional information immediately. And all of it can be linked to the recipients' personal profiles. This may allow email marketers to ask fewer questions when someone first signs up, and instead engage incrementally over time.

The ability to make purchases directly from within an email is improving rapidly as well. Some retailers have already implemented solutions where a click-to-buy link in the email encodes the product code and customer ID. Clicking on the link takes you to the retailer's website, identifies you, pulls up your purchase information (assuming you're a returning customer), and puts the product into your shopping cart. After entering a password and making a few more clicks, your order is in the mail. This level of integration between promotional emails and Web retailers is rapidly becoming the norm. In short, the interactivity provided on the website is going to become indistinguishable from the interactivity available from within email messages.

DATA TECHNOLOGIES

Databases are getting larger and larger, making it possible to store information with greater detail and create more complex data models. The technologies used to collect, consolidate, and analyze the data are improving rapidly, and so are the predictive models and technologies that can use the data to detect patterns and anticipate future behavior. The engaged organization is getting access to the data-driven tools that allow it to become smart about how it listens to and understands its customers.

WEB PERSONALIZATION

When you show up on a website, the engaged organization will immediately identify and recognize you. The pages you see on the site will be customized to present special offers and information targeted specifically to you. If you've chosen not to receive email, the same messages can still be linked in to the website, giving you the option to view them there instead.

INSTANT MESSAGING

Instant messaging (IM), sometimes called "online chat," is becoming an increasingly powerful way to engage customers. (Some IM functions can be automated, but the term generally implies interacting with a live person.) While there are often delays sending and receiving email, IM happens in real time. If a customer shows up on your website and needs help locating a product or specific information or is having difficulty navigating on the site, IM enables someone at your company to communicate directly with her. IM functionality may also become incorporated directly into email marketing programs. Emails may have embedded "Need Help?" and "Got Any Questions?" buttons that recipients can click on to immediately reach a customer service or salesperson. The customer's profile would instantly pop up on the service representative's screen, complete with a detailed history of all previous interactions with that customer and a snapshot of the email the customer is responding to.

VOICE AND TELEPHONY

Voice can be used in two ways to expand customer dialogue. The first is as an extension of instant messaging. While IM requires users to type in questions and responses, voice-enabled chat allows them to speak through what is basically a telephone function over the

Internet. Some customers may prefer typing, while others prefer talking. Adding a voice function to IM gives the customer a choice. A related variation on this is the callback function, which is becoming an increasingly common part of websites and email marketing programs. Customers who click a specific button will receive a call from a knowledgeable customer service person minutes later. And as email and voice mail become more and more integrated, consumers will be able to choose whether they would like to receive messages from an organization by voice mail or email.

WIRELESS TECHNOLOGIES

Devices such as Web-enabled cellular telephones, portable computing devices such as the Palm VII handheld, and wireless modems are making it increasingly possible to connect to the Internet from absolutely anywhere. Whether you're searching for information on a restaurant, getting directions to a meeting, sending a short message to a colleague, buying tickets on your way to the movies, looking up a friend's telephone number, or receiving alerts when a stock you're following hits a certain level and placing a quick trade, you'll be able to do it all with the new generation of handheld wireless devices.

WEB COLLABORATION

This technology (often integrated with IM functionality) enables a sales or support person to take control of the customer's Web browser and lead him to pages containing products and information he's interested in or help him use specific functions on the site. The customer and support person interact and communicate with each other, engaging in true, real-time dialogue.

VIDEO AND AUDIO

While most video on the Internet today is jerky and small and streaming audio playback is low-fidelity, it won't be long until audio and video will rival the quality we expect from our home entertainment systems. Noninteractive, streaming video, audio, and animation are nice ways to enhance static text, graphics, and images. They're also great ways to get people's attention and enhance their experience and involvement. And that's just the beginning.

In the case of audio, new technologies such as MP3 and Napster are already having a profound impact. Although most consumers cannot play music in real time on the Web without compromising quality and fidelity, high-quality audio can be downloaded and played from the computer hard disk. It is only a question of time until most of the music we listen to will be delivered on demand over the Internet. And when that happens companies will also discover new, creative ways to give their customers the option of receiving their messages in audio or as emails with music accompaniment.

When it comes to video, things are a bit different. In order to be truly effective as a part of the customer dialogue, the video experience will have to embrace a new model of interactivity, akin to tell-me-more television. But regardless, the creative use of new technologies will greatly enhance customers' experience of dialogue, particularly when it is seamlessly integrated.

USING NARRATIVE PRINCIPLES TO ENGAGE YOUR CUSTOMERS

One of the most powerful ways to teach and communicate is through stories. And one of the best ways to engage your customers is to think of your communications as a narrative. Even the blandest material can be spiced up by giving it an engaging rhythm and making it familiar and involving. At the same time, even the most exciting information can be made boring by presenting it as a list of facts, without any personality or tension. Like a good storyteller, you have to consider how your story will engage your audience. Now I'm not proposing that you try to disguise your marketing and sales messages as gripping drama. Customers are too savvy for that and they'll call your bluff. But you can still include a narrative thread to draw people in. An online health products retailer could, for example, includes a storyline in its email communication that features real people and the impact that health products have had on their lives. By following the lives of a cast of characters over an extended time period, readers become engaged in the story and follow it. The important thing to remember is that people like stories, remember them, and enjoy telling them to others.

USING EMOTION TO ENGAGE YOUR CUSTOMERS

The engaged customer has moved beyond having a casual connection with or simply being aware of your company. The engaged customer has developed an emotional connection to your company. What if you could plan for and factor that emotion into your customer communication? Is it even reasonable to speak about having a relationship with your customers if you are not taking into consideration their emotional connection with your brand and their emotional response to your communication? There are ways that the data you have about your customers can give you hints about their emotional disposition. We can predict what images and words will most likely strike a chord with them. Is using the knowledge that "emotional modeling" gives us a form of covert manipulation, or is it the same thing we all do when we interact with each other in the real world? If a salesperson is trying to sell you something, she'll probably pay close attention to your emotional response (at least if she's a good salesperson), and she'll modify her message accordingly. We will see comparable capabilities available to the e-marketer in the near future. For example, a company called Emotion Engine (www.emotionengine.com) is already in the process of developing technology that will enable companies to further personalize their customer communication by including emotional profiles.

USING "THE CAUSE" TO
ENGAGE YOUR CUSTOMERS

Cause-based marketing is a term that we are going to hear more about in the coming years. The Internet has made it possible for marketers to take cause-based marketing one step further, appealing to customers by linking their loyalty with support for their favorite cause. A corporation might, for instance, donate a percentage of the value of your purchase to your favorite charity or allow you to give your loyalty points to a favorite cause. According to United Airlines, the most successful mileage awards promotion they ever did allowed members to donate miles to Médicins sans Frontières, a nonprofit group of doctors who provide free medical care in war-torn and impoverished areas around the world. The Internet enables customers to directly access the companies they do business with and actively choose the cause or charity they want their money donated to. While offering a relatively small promotion to each customer, the aggregate impact for the receiving charity could be formidable. Schoolpop (www.schoolpop.com) is among a new breed of online services that let Internet users dedicate a significant portion of the revenue generated from their online activity (from browsing banner advertisements to making purchases) to a cause of their choosing. Cause-based marketing provides a powerful and compelling means for companies to appeal to high-value customer segments. I believe we have only seen the beginnings of a number of creative applications of cause-based marketing as a way of engaging customers to significantly increase their loyalty.

FROM INDIVIDUALIZED DIALOGUE TO INDIVIDUALIZED PRODUCT

Individualized dialogue is only the tip of the customization iceberg. The engaged organization of the future won't be limited to building relationships with its customers by implementing good customer service and communicating with individualized emails and websites. Every product or service they sell will be built to order. Booksellers will print books as you order them, including special covers and an introduction or greeting that you can write yourself. For several years now, Dell has enabled its customers to configure its new computers when buying them on the Web. Soon you will be able to build your own computer with even greater control, selecting its color, picking the software you want installed, and truly customizing the hardware setup. Within a few years people may no longer buy their cars at dealerships, instead "building" them on the Web, selecting the features they like and then picking it up at their local dealer. Or maybe they will sign up for that personalized automotive plan, mentioned earlier, that provides a four-wheel drive vehicle in the winter and a convertible in the summer. Products and services ranging from electronics to apparel to music to insurance policies to financial services will be customized and configured uniquely for each buyer. The implications for how companies must get to know their customers are far-reaching.

We have only seen the very beginning of the e-retailing revolution. Through mass customization the Web is going to live up to its full potential and truly demonstrate its power as a new retailing medium, allowing companies to sell products and services in ways they have never done before. Companies that invest in getting to know their customers as individuals today will be perfectly positioned to lead the mass customization revolution.

THE EMERGENCE OF NETWORKS
OF CUSTOMER INFORMATION

The Web is a great platform for a new and very different type of collective bargaining. Communities of individuals with shared interests or causes can engage a new breed of organization that has cropped up to represent and protect their interests. Sometimes these community organizations act as brokers or agents on their members' behalf. In their book *Net Gain* John Hagel III and Arthur G. Armstrong predicted the emergence of these organizations, calling them "information intermediaries" or "infomediaries."

Consider how American Express might act as an informediary for its credit card customers. Any company that wants to communicate with an Amex customer could do so either by working through Amex or by trying to reach the customers on its own—not knowing who they are. By electing to work with Amex, the company could reach members who have told Amex about specific interests or affiliations. Amex might, for instance, create a website where its customers could check card balance *and* register their current interests. Amex would not reveal this information directly to the company wanting to reach its members, but would instead make an introduction to its members on behalf of the company, leaving it up to individual members whether they choose to interact further.

Hagel and Armstrong also predict that groups of individuals will use infomediaries to help them bargain for special advantages, such as better pricing from vendors. One company built on this model is MobShop (www.mobshop.com). MobShop has created a network of websites that pools large numbers of buyers together from all over the Internet, enabling MobShop to negotiate limited-time large-volume discounts. As infomediaries become more common, engaging individual customers in direct dialogue will become far more challenging.

Companies such as DoubleClick and Engage are taking the idea of customer information networks in a different direction. These companies and others like them collect information across broad networks of online and offline sources and act as gatekeepers, providing or limiting access to the people in their networks. Nevertheless, these self-styled communications gateways are a generation or two away from being truly successful, mainly because they're operating their businesses based on principles from the traditional world of advertising and direct marketing: they're collecting information anonymously. To become true infomediaries these companies will need to invent new models that give consumers access to their own personal profiles while respecting—and protecting—their privacy.

Once a company joins a network, the information it contributes is worth more than if it had remained on its own. And as even more companies join, the value of their information grows exponentially. This dynamic is often referred to as the "network effect," and it also holds true for individual consumers banding together in communities. The future of customer dialogue will be heavily impacted by network effects. No organization will be able to afford *not* to participate in a network and share its data and information. Individuals will realize that they have more leverage and protection by pooling their personal information and participating in communities (networks of likeminded individuals) that represent their interests.

DATA AND PRIVACY: MORE EXPLOSIVE THAN EVER

As I have discussed, much of the future of the Internet economy hinges on the delicate balance between consumers' need for privacy and marketers' need for data and information. How would *you* feel if every credit card purchase you make, every website you visit, all the preferences and personal information you disclose, and every marketing email you have ever responded to are all gathered in one gigantic database? The question of whether this is a marketer's dream or a consumer privacy nightmare is never far from the surface. It certainly holds the potential for both.

Many businesses would love to see this scenario become a reality. And they would argue that consumers will actually benefit because they'll receive more personalized, and therefore more relevant, marketing messages. The problem is that the potential for abuse and violation of privacy is enormous. For example, if a journalist spends time investigating child pornography websites as background for a story, this information could become part of his personal profile. Ten years later, if that same journalist runs for election or gets involved in a child custody battle, his professionally motivated quest for information could resurface and be used against him.

While this is an "innocent" example, others might not be. What if someone was, in fact, visiting the pornography site with different motives. Do issues of free speech and freedom from unwarranted searches still apply? These are complex issues beyond the scope of this book. Suffice it to say that there will be significant regulatory developments over the coming years pertaining to online privacy rights.

There are two approaches being debated as privacy takes center stage in the public debate: industry self-regulation and government regulation.

INDUSTRY SELF-REGULATION

This is a bit of an oxymoron. If industry had one voice and one agenda, self-regulation might work. But in fiercely competitive, unregulated situations violations are inevitable and, in the absence of the rule of law, easily overlooked. As a result, all it takes to stir up fear and doubt among customers is a very small number of companies—or even a single one—crossing the line and violating consumer privacy.

In 1999, DoubleClick, the banner advertising network, acquired

Abacus Direct. Abacus owns and operates a database for the catalog marketing industry that contains purchase history on tens of millions of consumers. The combination of the Abacus database with DoubleClick's online tracking database caused online privacy organizations to file a formal complaint with the FTC for "unfair and deceptive business practices." In early 2000, a northern California resident filed suit against DoubleClick asking the court to prevent the company from "using technology to collect personal information from Internet users without their prior written consent." Although DoubleClick argues that what it is doing is neither illegal nor deceptive, the company has clearly touched a raw nerve. The DoubleClick-Abacus alliance will probably not be the last case of new Internet businesses attempting to harness data to improve the effectiveness of their marketing solutions. And this recent lawsuit won't be the last time consumer privacy advocates cry foul.

Perhaps the best attempts at industry self-regulation to date have been those of the Online Privacy Alliance (OPA), a coalition of industry groups. OPA's online privacy guidelines apply to information collected about consumers at the individual level and specify guidelines for disclosure, data security, and consumer access to their own information. The guidelines even call for self-enforcement mechanisms that provide consumers with adequate recourse. Although OPA's guidelines are fairly comprehensive, no one is quite sure how they'll be used and enforced. And as the DoubleClick example demonstrates, an industry built on a medium as new as the Internet can't possibly ensure that everyone plays fair—or even agree on what playing fair means.

GOVERNMENT REGULATION

The Internet industry currently has little confidence that governments can properly regulate the use of consumer information in a way that simultaneously takes industry concerns into consideration and serves the public good. At the same time, privacy advocates believe that the government should immediately step in to protect individuals' rights, which they believe are under attack from the Internet's new technologies and capabilities. These opposing camps are working out their differences in the press and in the courts and will be for some time to come.

Despite all the disagreement, though, some privacy cases are fairly straightforward. The Children's Online Privacy Protection Act, for example, which became law in 1998, is designed to protect children from possible threats and abuse associated with collecting and selling personal information. It requires, among other things, that an organization collecting information on a child under the age of 13 receive verifiable prior consent from the child's parents. This means that companies have to be extremely careful about how they collect and use information on a segment of the population that cannot look out for its own interests. It also makes it very difficult to collect that information in a cost-effective way.

Regardless of how one feels about government regulation, there's little doubt that it's better to be regulated by the federal government than by individual states. In Arkansas, for example, the state keeps lists of people who don't want to receive telemarketing calls. Making a call to someone on the list can result in a $10,000 fine. In California, legislators recently made it illegal for veterinarians to sell information about owners of pets that have had medical treatment. They also passed an antispam law, making it illegal to send unsolicited email unless it's properly labeled with key words in the message headers. Some states have even harsher protections; some have none at all. What seems clear, though, is that having a single set of federal laws that apply everywhere is a far more efficient and less confusing way to regulate a national—and global—industry.

Other countries are far more conservative in their approach to privacy. For example, the European Union Privacy Directive requires that any company doing business within the European Union get explicit approval from individuals in order to collect, store, and use information about them. Companies must describe how they intend to use the information and who will have access to it. The Privacy Directive is a baseline that every country in the EU must adhere to, but individual national governments may add even stricter protections. France, for instance, makes it nearly impossible to host databases containing information about French customers on non-French soil.

Inevitably, the government is going to end up regulating how customer information is used. The only questions are when and how much. To prepare yourself and your organization, make sure that you adhere to the best practices outlined in this book and that you stay within the OPA online privacy guidelines. Individuals and organizations alike will be best served in a world where full disclosure and full access to one's personal information is the law. What companies do with information they collect on their customers or how they collect it should not be regulated—provided, of course, that they tell people that they are collecting it, what they plan to do with it, and whether—and to whom—they plan to sell it. In short, companies must be required to give customers ownership of their personal the information through full access to and control of their individual profiles.

As I write the final words of this book in seat 7D on yet another United flight I am experiencing the reason why I have become a loyal United customer. And it is not just due to the free travel that all my mileage plus points have earned me. The reason I keep returning to United is that my loyalty has earned me the benefit of exclusive service. I am a good customer. In fact I am a highly profitable customer. In return, they offer me perks and special privileges that make my life just a little bit simpler and a lot more comfortable. I am prioritized in the upgrade queue, I get lots of free upgrade certificates and priority boarding (I always know there'll be room in the overhead bin for my rollon bag). Sometimes I even get priority meal selection, meaning that on full flights they won't run out of chicken before they get to me. Occasionally the flight attendants will look me up on their list and thank me for my loyalty. And to help simplify my life even a little bit more, United even sends me an email if a flight I'm scheduled for has been delayed. It all adds up. I have become an engaged United customer not because of any one thing they do for me, but because they demonstrate that they know me and offer relevant service. None of this costs United very much at all, but it's this extra service that makes it worth my while to arrange my schedule around their departure times and sometimes even their flight routes.

The other day eBags sent me a colorful camera in the mail as a thank you for purchases I had made with them in the past year. It was a cool-looking little camera, but even more important, it was a very nice gesture that made me feel appreciated and recognized as a customer. A few days later I received an email from eBags telling me that the line of luggage that I had purchased was going out of production. They wanted to know if I had any interest in buying any of the pieces I hadn't added to my "collection" yet?

Just as United offers me special benefits and eBags recognizes me with a small gift, we all want to be recognized and treated as the special individuals we are. While there is a growing awareness about the importance of building lasting relationships with customers, I hope that this book has helped you gain a better understanding that service-oriented communication and recognition at the individual level will make those relationships truly flourish. And there is no better way to communicate with each customer as an individual than through the incredible power of the Internet. How and what you choose to say is naturally going to depend on your business and your brand. Issues ranging from cost and resource constraints and organizational obstacles to privacy concerns can make building a service-oriented marketing program a formidable challenge. But the value to your customers and members and the resulting benefit to your organization from a program done right will make it all worthwhile. Profitability and sustainability of all Internet business hinges on engaged customers, and there couldn't be a more perfect time to seize the opportunity to get engaged with them than today.

INDEX

DILBERT reprinted by permission of United Feature Syndicate, Inc.